NO-FEAR

HOME
improvement

CREATIVE HOMEOWNER®

NO-FEAR

HOME
improvement

CREATIVE HOMEOWNER®, Upper Saddle River, New Jersey

NO-FEAR HOME IMPROVEMENTS

MANAGING EDITOR	Fran J. Donegan
SENIOR GRAPHIC DESIGN COORDINATOR	Glee Barre
PHOTO RESEARCHER	Robyn Poplasky
EDITORIAL ASSISTANT	Nora Grace, Jennifer Calvert
INDEXER	Schroeder Indexing Services
COVER DESIGN	David Geer
FRONT COVER PHOTOGRAPHY	Clockwise from top left: Merle Henkenius; John Parsekian/CH; Brian C. Nieves/CH; John Parsekian/CH
BACK COVER PHOTOGRAPHY	John Parsekian/CH

CREATIVE HOMEOWNER

VICE PRESIDENT AND PUBLISHER	Timothy O. Bakke
PRODUCTION DIRECTOR	Kimberly H. Vivas
ART DIRECTOR	David Geer
MANAGING EDITOR	Fran J. Donegan

Current Printing (last digit)
10 9 8 7 6 5 4 3 2 1

No-Fear Home Improvement, First Edition
Library of Congress Control Number: 2007922562
ISBN-10: 1-58011-368-0
ISBN-13: 978-1-58011-368-7
CREATIVE HOMEOWNER®
A Division of Federal Marketing Corp.
24 Park Way
Upper Saddle River, NJ 07458
www.creativehomeowner.com

Safety

Although the methods in this book have been reviewed for safety, it is not possible to over-state the importance of using the safest methods you can. What follows are reminders—some do's and don'ts of work safety—to use along with your common sense.

◆ Always use caution, care, and good judgment when following the procedures described in this book.

◆ Always be sure that the electrical setup is safe, that no circuit is overloaded, and that all power tools and outlets are properly grounded. Do not use power tools in wet locations.

◆ Always read container labels on paints, sol-vents, and other products; provide ventilation; and observe all other warnings.

◆ Always read the manufacturer's instructions for using a tool, especially the warnings.

◆ Use hold-downs and push sticks whenever possible when working on a table saw. Avoid working short pieces if you can.

◆ Always remove the key from any drill chuck (portable or press) before starting the drill.

◆ Always pay deliberate attention to how a tool works so that you can avoid being injured.

◆ Always know the limitations of your tools. Do not try to force them to do what they were not designed to do.

◆ Always make sure that any adjustment is locked before proceeding. For example, always check the rip fence on a table saw or the bevel adjustment on a portable saw before starting to work.

◆ Always clamp small pieces to a bench or other work surface when using a power tool.

◆ Always wear the appropriate rubber gloves or work gloves when handling chemicals, moving or stacking lumber, working with concrete, or doing heavy construction.

◆ Always wear a disposable face mask when you create dust by sawing or sanding. Use a spe-cial filtering respirator when working with toxic substances and solvents.

◆ Always wear eye protection, especially when using power tools or striking metal on metal or concrete; a chip can fly off, for example, when chiseling concrete.

◆ Never work while wearing loose clothing, open cuffs, or jewelry; tie back long hair.

◆ Always be aware that there is seldom enough time for your body's reflexes to save you from injury from a power tool in a dangerous situa-tion; everything happens too fast. Be alert!

◆ Always keep your hands away from the busi-ness ends of blades, cutters, and bits.

◆ Always hold a circular saw firmly, usually with both hands.

◆ Always use a drill with an auxiliary han-dle to control the torque when using large-size bits.

◆ Always check your local building codes when planning new construction. The codes are intended to protect public safety and should be observed to the letter.

◆ Never work with power tools when you are tired or when under the influence of alcohol or drugs.

◆ Never cut tiny pieces of wood or pipe using a power saw. When you need a small piece, saw it from a securely clamped longer piece.

◆ Never change a saw blade or a drill or router bit unless the power cord is unplugged. Do not depend on the switch being off. You might acciden-tally hit it.

◆ Never work in insufficient lighting.

◆ Never work with dull tools. Have them sharp-ened, or learn how to sharpen them yourself.

◆ Never use a power tool on a workpiece—large or small—that is not firmly supported.

◆ Never saw a workpiece that spans a large distance between horses without close support on each side of the cut; the piece can bend, closing on and jamming the blade, causing saw kickback.

◆ When sawing, never support a work-piece from underneath with your leg or other part of your body.

◆ Never carry sharp or pointed tools, such as utility knives, awls, or chisels, in your pocket. If you want to carry any of these tools, use a special-purpose tool belt that has leather pockets and holders.

Table of Contents

About this Book

Some people are afraid of flying, some are afraid of snakes, and some are afraid of taking on even the simplest home-repair or improvement project. We can't do much for the first two groups, but those who suffer from "repairaphobia" are about to get some relief. *No-Fear Home Improvement* takes the fear factor out of owning and maintaining a home. The book removes the fear of spending too much money, the fear of looking or sounding foolish in front of the repairman, and the fear of making the problem worse, which may be the biggest fear of all.

The book covers over 100 small projects and repairs that have the potential to drive most people crazy. *No-Fear Home Improvement* provides the information—and the confidence—to stop leaky faucets, quiet running toilets, and repair the small rip in the screen on the back door, among others.

The first chapter explains how the systems in your house work together and helps you cope with emergency situations. The second chapter introduces you to the simple tools you'll need to make the repairs. The last six chapters are filled with the type of projects that every homeowner encounters from time to time. They cover simple repairs, painting, electrical, plumbing, and making improvements.

The instructions are easy to understand, and each project is complete with photos or illustrations that emphasis the important information. In addition to the main projects, you'll find sidebars and "Smart Tips, "examples of which are shown to the right, throughout the book. They provide extra bits of information that will help you purchase the right material, select the right tool, or complete your project.

SAFETY

Pneumatic nailers may be advanced for beginners, but don't be afraid of them. They are real labor savers, and you can usually rent them. They have a lock-out device that won't let you fire the tool unless the head is held firmly against a board.

SMART TIP

Don't discard the directions or the wiring schematic (the wire routing map) that comes in the box. Keep it on hand in case there is a problem at a later date.

Painting Projects

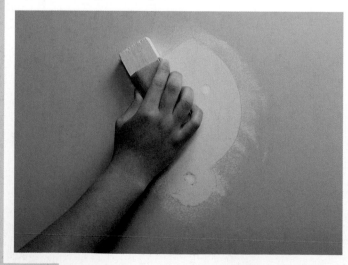

Repairs and Maintenance

Electrical Projects

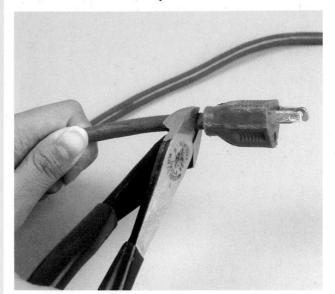

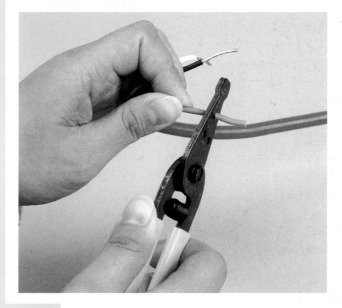

Plumbing Projects

Making Improvements

1
Understanding Your House

Explaining Plumbing

I f you look below, you will see the typical route water takes from the street or private well to sinks, tubs, and other plumbing fixtures. Most piping is made of copper, but plastic material (CPVC) is gaining in popularity. A drain and waste system is shown opposite. Drains work through a combination of gravity and air that serves to equalize the pressure in the system. You can deal with minor clogs, but call a plumber to inspect a faulty drainage system. (See Chapter 5, "Plumbing Projects," page 64.)

Water- Supply Lines

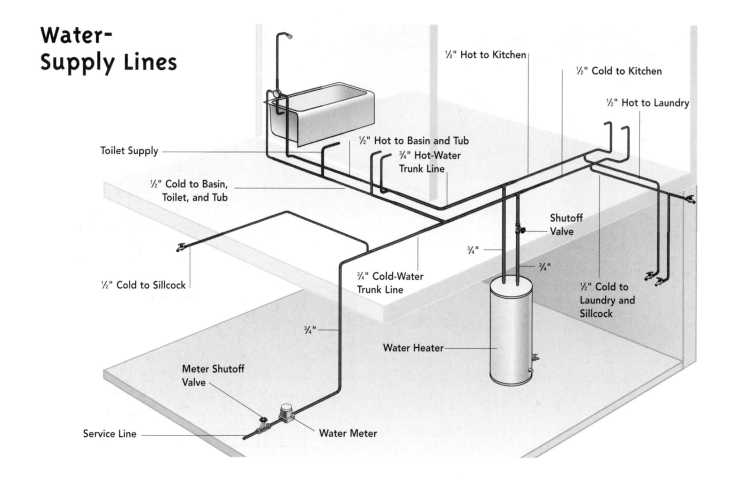

½" Hot to Kitchen

½" Cold to Kitchen

½" Hot to Laundry

½" Hot to Basin and Tub

¾" Hot-Water Trunk Line

Toilet Supply

½" Cold to Basin, Toilet, and Tub

Shutoff Valve

¾"

¾"

½" Cold to Sillcock

¾" Cold-Water Trunk Line

¾"

½" Cold to Laundry and Sillcock

¾"

Water Heater

Meter Shutoff Valve

Service Line

Water Meter

No Basement?

Where are the water pipes if you live in a house without a basement? It depends on the type of home. If your ground floor spans a crawl space, the piping is likely to resemble that of a basement installation, except that the water heater may be located on the main floor in a utility closet.

If yours is a slab-on-grade home with a concrete floor, expect to find soft-copper water piping buried under the concrete slab. The water service in this case will usually enter a utility room through the floor. In most cases, the fixture supply piping will also be run under the slab, surfacing in the utility room near the meter on one end, and near each fixture or group of fixtures on the other. In the extreme southern reaches of the country, where hard freezes are unlikely, copper or plastic water lines may be run in the attic, with branch lines dropping into plumbing walls throughout the house.

Whole-House Drain and Vent System

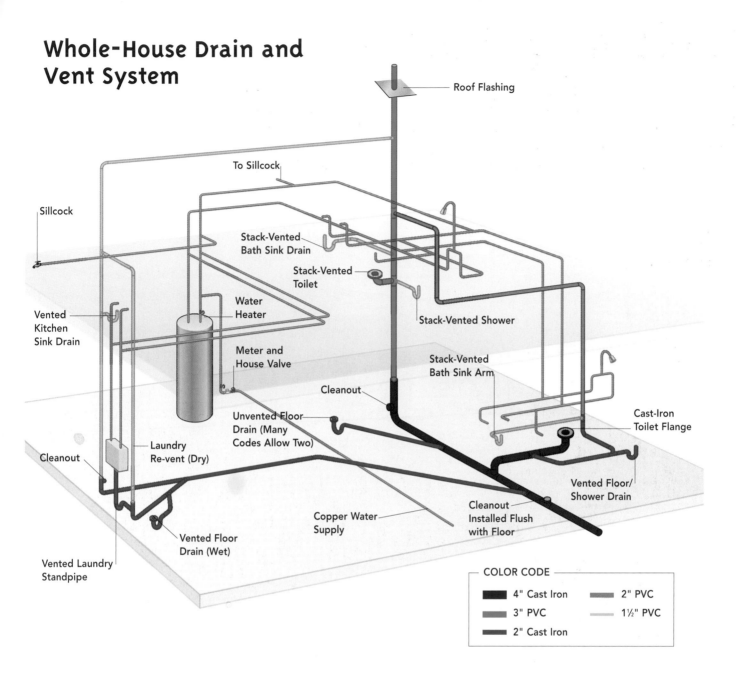

Roof Flashing

To Sillcock

Sillcock

Stack-Vented
Bath Sink Drain

Stack-Vented
Toilet

Vented
Kitchen
Sink Drain

Water
Heater

Stack-Vented Shower

Meter and
House Valve

Stack-Vented
Bath Sink Arm

Cleanout

Cast-Iron
Toilet Flange

Unvented Floor
Drain (Many
Codes Allow Two)

Cleanout

Laundry
Re-vent (Dry)

Vented Floor/
Shower Drain

Copper Water
Supply

Vented Floor
Drain (Wet)

Cleanout
Installed Flush
with Floor

Vented Laundry
Standpipe

COLOR CODE		
■ 4" Cast Iron	■ 2" PVC	
■ 3" PVC	■ 1½" PVC	
■ 2" Cast Iron		

Shutoff Valves

Before making any kind of plumbing repair, turn off the water. You can usually to this by closing the in-line shutoff valve that should be installed near all fixtures, such as sinks and toilets. If they are not there, have a plumber install them. There's also a main valve where the outside waterline enters your home. Learn the location of shutoff valves in the home.

This type of valve is usually found near toilets or under the sink.

Pull this lever perpendicular to the pipe to stop the flow of water.

The Secrets of Electricity

When electrical power enters your home it goes through a meter—that's how the utility knows what to charge you—and then to a distribution point. In older homes, the distribution point is a fuse box; in newer homes, it is a service-entrance panel, but most people call it a circuit-breaker or panel box. The end use of the electricity determines the size of the wires and the amount of power needed, measured in amps and volts. Look at the panel box in your home. Each breaker controls an electric circuit and is stamped with a number. The list below matches amps with types of circuits. The illustration shows how the different circuits travel throughout the home. (See Chapter 6, "Electrical Projects," page 92.)

Circuit Anatomy

120 volts, 20 amps – disposal

120/240 volts, 60 amps – range

120 volts, 20 amps – small appliances

120 volts, 15 amps – lights

240 volts, 20 amps – basement heater

120/240 volts, 30 amps – dryer

240 volts, 30 amps – water heater

ground

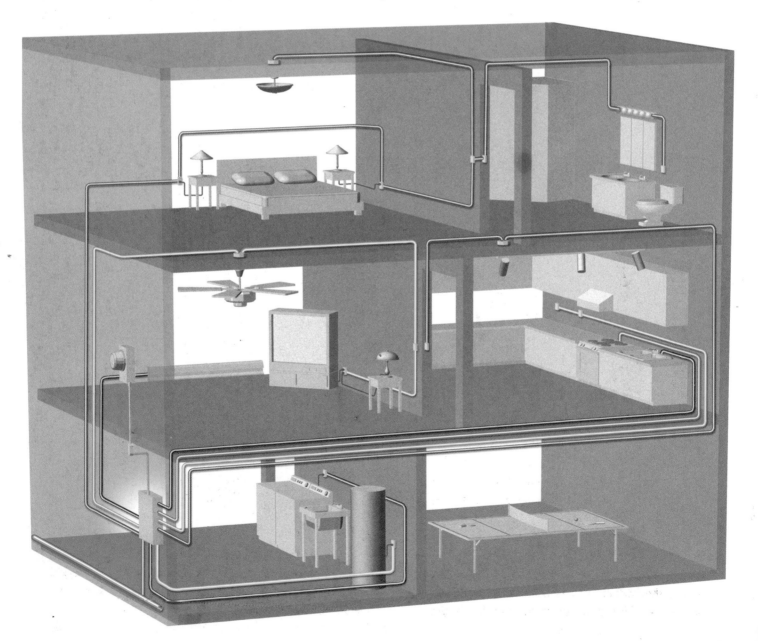

Checking for Damage

You can easily diagnose a blown fuse element by looking through the fuse glass. A burned element suggests an overload; a broken element and darkened glass suggests a short circuit.

When a plug fuse is blown, the fuse shell may also be damaged. Check it for signs of burning and arcing.

A damaged plug fuse will clearly show marks caused by burning and arcing.

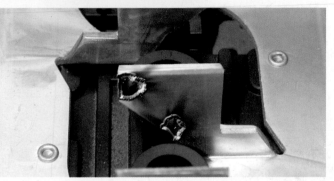

Burn flashes in a circuit breaker panel are a telltale sign of serious damage.

SMART TIP

If you reset a circuit breaker and it immediately trips again, an overload or faulty wiring problem persists. So, don't force the breaker into the "on" position.

Service Entrance Panel, or "Breaker Box"

Here's what a panel box looks like with the cover off. The large black and red wires carry electricity into the home from the outside. The breaker to which they are attached can cut the power to the entire house. The large silver wire on the right is the neutral and is the third wire you see entering your home. The wires attached to the other breakers carry power throughout your home. The black ones carry the power; the white wires complete the circuit; the bare copper wires ground the system. If there is an overload on a circuit, the breaker will trip, cutting power to the circuit.

Hot Bus

Neutral Bus

Grounding Bus

The ends of the white and bare wires get connected to what is called a bus bar. The ends of the black wires are connected to the breakers.

Dealing with Home Emergencies

Be Prepared

Not every emergency can be prepared for, but if you live in an area prone to hurricanes, floods, earthquakes, or tornadoes, you should have basic emergency supplies on hand, and your family should be aware of what steps to take when disaster strikes.

Hurricanes. The National Hurricane Center recommends that those living in low-lying areas have an evacuation plan. Find out about the best routes from your local police or Red Cross chapter. Also plan for emergency communication, such as contacting a friend out of the storm area, in case family members are separated. Listen to the radio or TV for warnings; check your emergency supplies, and fuel the car. Bring in outdoor objects

such as lawn furniture, and close shutters or install plywood before the storm arrives. Unplug appliances, cut off the main circuit breaker, and turn off the main water-supply valve.

Tornadoes. Have a place ready where you can take shelter—if you don't have a basement, find a windowless spot on the ground floor, such as a bathroom or a closet under stairs. As tornadoes usually happen with little warning, know the danger signs.

Earthquakes. If you live in an earthquake zone, have all shelves fastened securely to your walls, and store heavy or breakable items close to the floor. During an earthquake, the safest place in your home (according to FEMA) is under a piece of heavy furniture or against an inside wall, away from windows or furniture that may topple.

Survival Tips. If you plan to ride out a storm, have basic emergency supplies on hand, including flashlights and extra batteries, a battery-operated radio, first-aid kit, extra nonperishable food and water, and essential medicines. Turn the refrigerator to its coldest setting, and open and close it only when absolutely necessary. Store drinking water in jugs and bottles—and in clean bathtubs.

Storms

Severe storms are quantified by their potential for damage.

Temporary Roof Repairs. It's natural to try to patch an active leak but unwise to work on a wet roof in bad weather. There are exceptions: mainly, if the house has a low-sloped or flat roof that you wouldn't roll off even if you slipped. When you can work safely, temporarily stem roof leaks using roof cement (not roof coating). On standard shingles, flashing, roll roofing, and even built-up flat roofs, pry apart the leaking seam, and fill the opening with the thick tar. Then, push the shingle seam or flashing edge back in place, and add another

thick layer of tar. If a shingle tab (the exposed section) has blown off, cover the area with tar, particularly exposed nailheads on the shingle layers below, and weave in a cover layer—if you don't have spare shingles, a piece of tarpaper or even a plastic bag will work just be sure to overlap them.

Clearing Bottlenecks. To help prevent damage, it pays to regularly check and clear gutters and downspouts—particularly the S-shaped offset fitting that directs water from roof overhangs back toward the building leader board. These fittings typically are held in place with sheet-metal screws, which you need to remove to gain access for cleaning that section of downspout.

To prevent gutters and drains from becoming laden with ice during the winter, you can install UL-approved electric heat cables. These are equipped with built-in thermostats that trigger a power flow when temperatures drop to the freezing point, keeping the gutters flowing.

Floods

The natural impulse after your house is flooded is to remove as much water as quickly as you can. But after a major flood, you should resist the impulse, and drain the water slowly.

Pumping Out Water. The hidden danger is that the ground outside the foundation wall is saturated and pressing against the masonry with the potential force of a mudslide. In extreme cases, several feet of water inside the wall pressing in the opposite direction may be the only thing preventing a collapse. According to the Federal Emergency Management Agency (FEMA), you should wait until water on the ground outside begins to drain away before pumping out the basement. Even then, you should reduce

the level only 2 or 3 feet the first day. Remember, don't use a gasoline-powered generator or pump inside the house because it releases deadly carbon monoxide fumes.

Sump Pumps. Check your sump pump; it can prevent major damage from flooding. Many models turn on when a float rises along a wire as water rises in the sump hole. If the sump has not kicked in recently, the float can

seize in place. Run it up and down a few times to make sure that the sump, and everything else, won't wind up submerged.

Foundation Repairs. Interior surface patches won't work on foundations because leaks have a wall of water behind them—sometimes massive hydrostatic pressure from a yard of compacted dirt that has turned to mud. But there is one material, hydraulic cement, that has the potential to stem an active leak through masonry. The dense cement mix should be forced into wet cracks, packed in layer after layer, and held in place with a cover board. Even if water continues to flow, the mix will harden and swell as it sets up. If you pack the crack tightly, the swelling mix fills nooks and crannies and can stop the leak.

Fire Safety

The most important fire protection is a working smoke detector. Next is a fully charged ABC-rated extinguisher that you can use against any type of home fire. For fireplaces and stoves, use a special chimney extinguisher. Most look like a road flare. You remove a striking cap, ignite the stick, and toss it into the fireplace or wood stove. It can suppress a fire in the chimney by displacing oxygen needed for combustion with a large volume of incombustible gas.

Smoke Detectors. If your smoke detectors are battery-powered, change the batteries on a set schedule. There are also hard-wired smoke detectors that run off house current (with battery back-ups). Install at least one smoke detector

on every level of the home.

Chimneys. Have a chimney sweep inspect chimneys, even if you use a fireplace only occasionally. Sweeps have the tools to dislodge hardened creosote, a by-product of incomplete combustion that can reignite and start fires. You can make an unlined flue safer with one of the masonry mix systems that forms a fire-safe shell inside the flue or by running code-approved

exhaust ducts through the chimney.

Extinguishers. Mount extinguishers near points where fires may start—one in the kitchen and one at the entrance to the utility room that houses a gas-fired furnace, water heater, and clothes dryer. Check the pressure dials to make sure extinguishers are charged.

Escape Routes. For maximum safety, particularly with children in the house, make sure you establish an evacuation plan with two ways out of every room, and walk children through the routes so they know what to do in an emergency.

Emergency Numbers. Post telephone numbers of local fire, police, and emergency services. Use an extinguisher against small, spot fires, but don't try to fight large, developing fires; leave the house.

2
Basic Tools and Fasteners

The Basic Tool Kit

It will cost you around $150 to assemble a good tool kit. (Splurge and get a multi-tier toolbox to hold it.) That $150 is what you'd pay a plumber to fix a single leak, so the money is well spent. And you will find that a well-made tool really does make the job go easier. The tools shown on the next few pages are suggestions of those in which you should invest, but you don't need to buy them all right away. Let the job determine the tools you purchase. And there really are differences among the different types of hammers, saws, and wrenches. You'll see the differences once you gain a little experience.

Wrenches

Ratchets provide leverage for tightening and loosening nuts and certain types of screws.

There are dozens of adjustable wrench designs, but the classic crescent will handle small and large jobs.

For heavy-duty plumbing work, a Stilson wrench with serrated jaws provides the most turning power.

Pliers

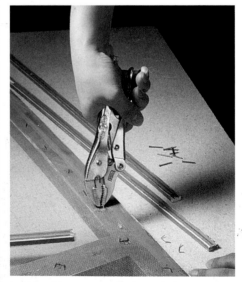

Use locking pliers (such as Vise-Grip or Robo-Grip brands) to securely grab what you're turning.

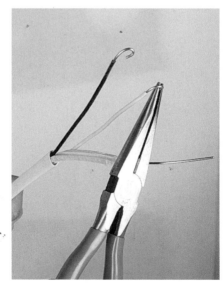

Long-nose pliers is mainly an electrician's tool but is handy for detail work in tight places.

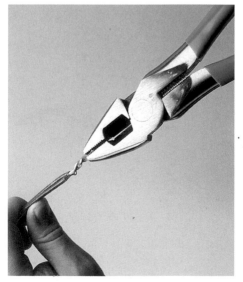

An electrician's or lineman's pliers is the most useful for wiring work. It can twist wires and cut through cable.

Saws

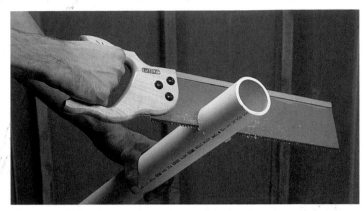

There are specialized trim saws and rip saws, but crosscut saws with 7 or 8 teeth per in. are the most versatile. The more teeth the finer the cut.

Short, stiff backsaws have fine teeth for detail and trim work. The teeth are not splayed, so the saw kerf is very narrow.

Drivers

In the basic screwdriver collection, you need a flat tip and a Phillips tip. Two sizes of each will handle most screws.

The nut driver, a pint-sized alternative to a full set of socket wrenches, will handle nuts and bolt threads for most appliances.

Hammers

The basic claw hammer is the most versatile model for DIY repairs and home improvement projects.

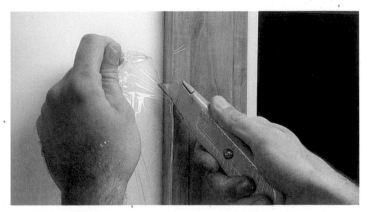

A utility knife handles everything from cutting drywall and batts of insulation to trimming molding edges.

Nails and Nailing

The simple nail isn't so simple. There are dozens of types to choose from, and you will find that it is important to select the right nail for the job—for example, a large masonry nail that is designed for use in concrete would obliterate a delicate piece of wood molding. Because nails are inexpensive, keep a good selection on hand, with a big box of 10d bright common nails as the workhorse of your nailing operation. Don't worry about the "d" attached to nail sizes. It used to refer to how many nails of that size you could get for a penny, but those days are long gone. The chart opposite shows nail sizes. Unless you buy in bulk, most nails are now sold in boxes that tell you the type of nail and its length.

SAFETY

Pneumatic nailers may be advanced for beginners, but don't be afraid of them. They are real labor savers, and you can usually rent them. They have a lock-out device that won't let you fire the tool unless the head is held firmly against a board.

Nail Sizes

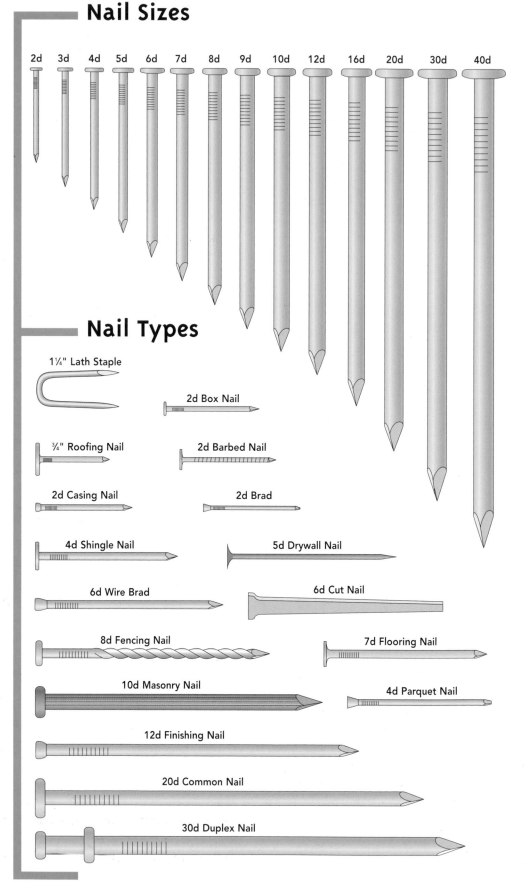

2d 3d 4d 5d 6d 7d 8d 9d 10d 12d 16d 20d 30d 40d

Nail Types

1¼" Lath Staple

2d Box Nail

¾" Roofing Nail

2d Barbed Nail

2d Casing Nail

2d Brad

4d Shingle Nail

5d Drywall Nail

6d Wire Brad

6d Cut Nail

8d Fencing Nail

7d Flooring Nail

10d Masonry Nail

4d Parquet Nail

12d Finishing Nail

20d Common Nail

30d Duplex Nail

Weights

TYPE OF NAIL	NAILS/LB.
3d box (1¼")	635
6d box (2")	236
10d box (3")	94
4d casing (1½")	473
8d casing (2½")	145
2d common (1")	876
4d common (1½")	316
6d common (2")	181
8d common (2½")	106
10d common (3")	69
12d common (3¼")	63
16d common (3½")	49
2d roofing (1")	255
6d roofing (2")	138

SMART TIP

Here's a rookie error you can easily avoid: if your wood splits when you nail it, don't blame the wood, look for a solution. The wood may be splitting because you're using a nail that's too wide. Try a thinner nail. Working with hardwood? These woods tend to be dense and split rather than give during nailing. Drill a pilot hole that's half as wide as the nail you're going to use to avoid splitting the wood.

Toenailing

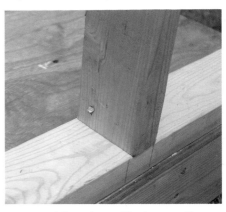

Toenailing lets you attach boards at a 90-deg. angle. Start at an angle about an inch from the joint.

As you drive the nail, steepen the angle slightly. Toenailing is usually used for rough carpentry only.

One-Hand Nailing

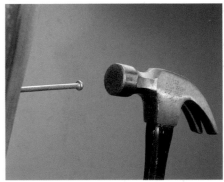

When you don't have the helper or the extra clamps you need, try this carpenter's trick of one-hand nailing.

Hold the head squarely against the side of your hammer to set the point; then drive the nail home.

Cat's Paw Pulling

Remove nails with minimal damage by driving the forked end of a cat's paw under the nailhead.

Rotate the cat's-paw handle to raise the nailhead, and finish pulling it out using the claw of your hammer.

Screws

They may all look the same to you, but screws are specialty fasteners that come in a variety of types, and each has attributes, such as thread configuration, that are designed for specific applications. For example, a wood screw has a different thread pattern and holding ability than a particleboard screw. If you used a drywall screw—which has low sheer strength but good resistance to pull out—to hold together furniture, you'll soon be sitting among a pile of kindling. The screwdriver is the basic tool used here, but a cordless drill/driver, see below, really speeds up the work.

Holding

Cordless drill/drivers are good for drilling but sometimes hard to use to control driving screws. That's where an extension holder will help. These tube-shaped attachments fit into the drill chuck, and can be fitted with different driving tips. To keep the tip engaged and drive screws in a straight line, the tube extends over the screw head and along its shank. The tube withdraws as you seat the screws.

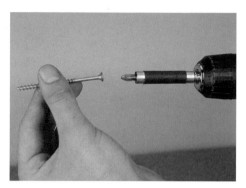

Tighten the driver attachment in the drill chuck, and fit one of the driving tips onto the screwhead.

You can let go of the screw because the driver head is magnetized; then, slide the guide tube over the shank.

Countersinking

A countersink is a shallow, conical hole that allows a screwhead to sit flush in the wood surface. This is a standard feature of screwed connections, and typically requires two bits. First, you need a pilot hole for the screw shank. Second, you need a countersink for the screwhead. Countersink bits do both jobs in one pass. You can adjust drilling depth using a collar on the bit.

A combination bit has a blade tip that carves a hole for the screw and a secondary cutter to make a countersink.

Most countersink bits have an adjustable collar so that you can control the depth and size of the recess.

Extracting

When you need to remove a screw and the turning slot is damaged or stripped bare, most people resort to pliers to try and grab just enough metal to start backing out a screw. When you can't, use a screw extractor bit. Bore a small hole in the screwhead, and turn in a specially spiraled extractor bit that tightens when you turn it to the left instead of to the right. Once it seats, continue turning to back out a screw.

To extract a screw with a damaged head, drill a pilot hole in the head that matches the extractor bit's diameter.

You can turn the extractor bit using a drill. When its reverse threads take hold, the damaged screw backs out.

Heads and Washers

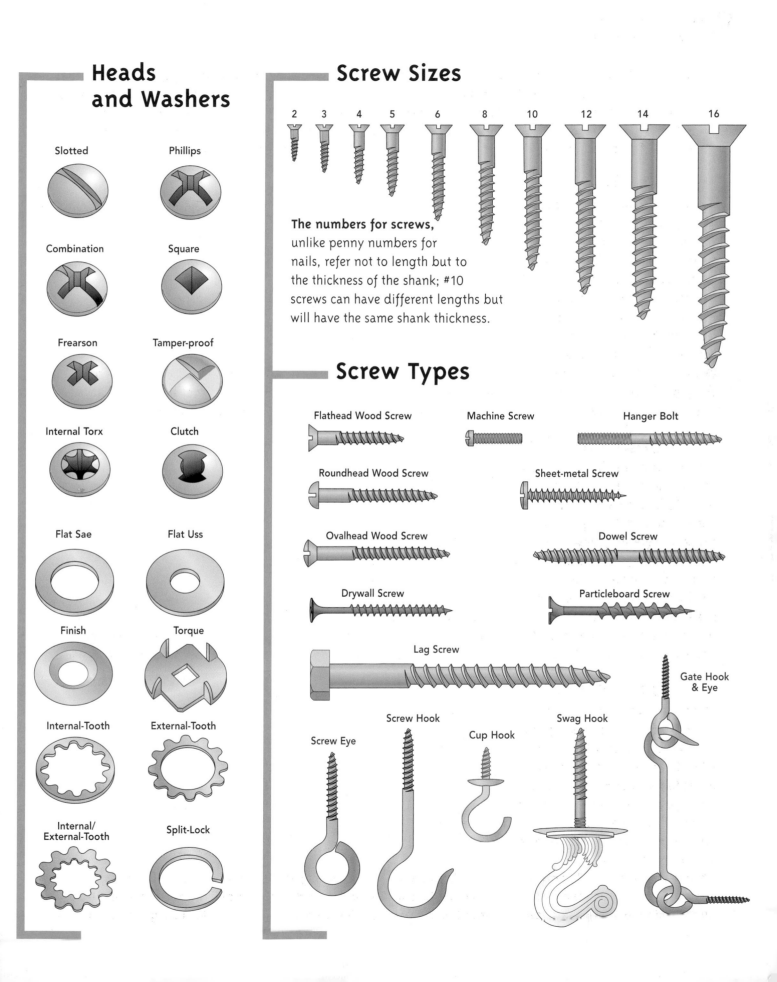

Slotted

Phillips

Combination

Square

Frearson

Tamper-proof

Internal Torx

Clutch

Flat Sae

Flat Uss

Finish

Torque

Internal-Tooth

External-Tooth

Internal/External-Tooth

Split-Lock

Screw Sizes

2   3   4   5   6   8   10   12   14   16

The numbers for screws, unlike penny numbers for nails, refer not to length but to the thickness of the shank; #10 screws can have different lengths but will have the same shank thickness.

Screw Types

Flathead Wood Screw

Machine Screw

Hanger Bolt

Roundhead Wood Screw

Sheet-metal Screw

Ovalhead Wood Screw

Dowel Screw

Drywall Screw

Particleboard Screw

Lag Screw

Screw Eye

Screw Hook

Cup Hook

Swag Hook

Gate Hook & Eye

Other Fasteners

There is a variety of other fasteners for use around the home. Unlike screws, bolts do not cut through material, and they need nuts to hold them in place. When installing a bolt, predrill a hole the same size as the bolt. When drilling a pilot holes for a screw, the hole should be smaller than the shank of the screw. Other household fasteners are shown at the bottom of the page. Use frame or hollow-wall fasteners when there isn't solid wood, such as a wood stud inside a wall, to grip the threads of a screw. Use them to hang shelves, window-treatment hardware, and the like.

Fine Threads

The difference between standard threads and fine threads is significant in some applications—for example, where you need maximum holding power between metal components. It may not be important for most of your projects, but if you want the highest possible strength on critical repairs, fine threads provide it by creating more interlocked surfaces between male and female threads.

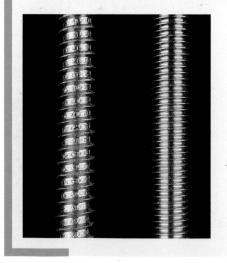

Bolts and Nuts

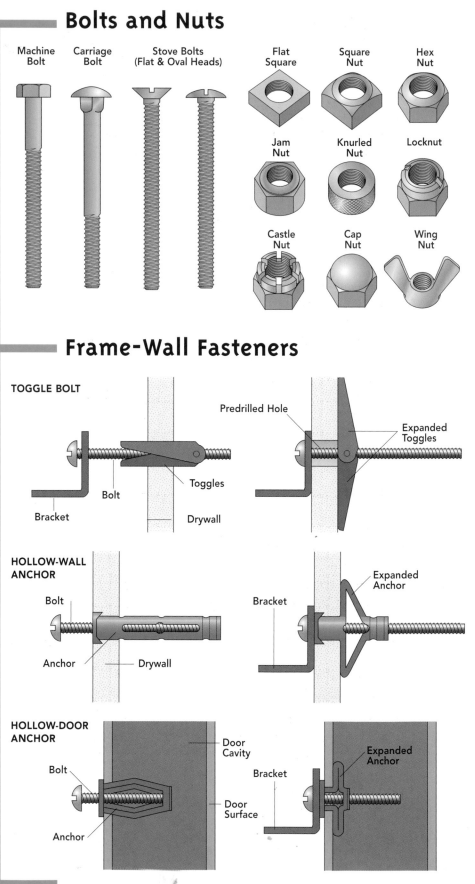

Machine Bolt

Carriage Bolt

Stove Bolts (Flat & Oval Heads)

Flat Square

Square Nut

Hex Nut

Jam Nut

Knurled Nut

Locknut

Castle Nut

Cap Nut

Wing Nut

Frame-Wall Fasteners

TOGGLE BOLT

Predrilled Hole

Expanded Toggles

Bracket

Bolt

Toggles

Drywall

HOLLOW-WALL ANCHOR

Bolt

Expanded Anchor

Bracket

Anchor

Drywall

HOLLOW-DOOR ANCHOR

Door Cavity

Expanded Anchor

Bolt

Bracket

Anchor

Door Surface

Locking

In most cases you can tighten nuts enough using a wrench or ratchet. But on installations subject to regular use and vibration, such as garage door tracks, there are two ways to add security. Either coat the bolt threads with an adhesive agent such as Locktite, loosening the nut later if need be, or coat the nut with silicone caulk, which also helps prevent corrosion.

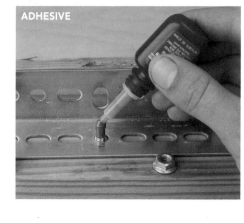

ADHESIVE

SILICONE

Loosening

Some nuts and bolts won't come apart no matter how much leverage you apply. In those cases, try breaking the corrosion with a penetrating lubricant. Another option is to break the rust bond by impact, using one hammer below the nut so the bolt won't bend, and another striking from above.

OIL

TWO HAMMERS

Removing

When lubricants and hammering won't budge the nut off a bolt, use a hacksaw. But rather than trying to saw through the bolt shank (and possibly damage the surface underneath), cut through one of the facets on the nut. This weakens the nut so that you can twist off the remaining section with a wrench.

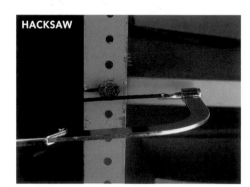

HACKSAW

WRENCH

Splitting

As a last resort, you can free a frozen nut—the kind you might find on a rusted bracket— using a nut splitter. First, fit the head of this hardened tool over the nut, and tighten down its splitting wedge by hand. Then, use a wrench or ratchet to drive the wedge into the side of the nut. This pressure will crack the nut.

SPLITTER

CUT

3
Painting Projects

Before You Paint

Painting is one of those activities that seems easy when you're watching someone else is do it. Hitting a golf ball seems easy, but few of us can hit a ball as well as Tiger Woods. So what turns the weekend golfer into a pro? You won't find the answer here. But you will learn the secret to a pro-quality paint job—and that secret is surface preparation. Take the time and exert the effort to clean and repair all surfaces, see below and opposite, to achieve a first-class paint job.

SMART TIP

GETTING RID OF MOLD AND MILDEW

Mold feeds on moisture and eventually forms gray-green spots that bleed through paint. Damp areas are susceptible to mold formation. Get rid of mold before painting using a solution of household bleach and water with a non-ammonia detergent. (Never mix ammonia and bleach.) Soap or detergent solution alone won't kill mold. Allow it to soak into the mold for 15 minutes before scrubbing and rinsing.

Spot-Painting Repairs

tools and materials

◆ Spackling or Joint compound ◆ Paint scraper
◆ Paintbrush ◆ Paint roller and tray ◆ Primer
◆ Paint ◆ Sandpaper ◆ Sanding block

1 Fill nailholes and small dents with lightweight joint compound. Leave a slight mound—the compound shrinks as it dries.

2 Use 150-grit sandpaper to sand down the dry joint compound until it is flush with the wall surface.

3 Because joint compound absorbs paint differently than drywall, prime the patched area before topcoating.

4 Roll paint onto the patch, and work the topcoat across the area. Keep a wet edge on the paint to avoid leaving ridges.

5 Smooth out the edges of the new paint with light, lifting strokes. To cover, you may need to repeat this process.

Testing for Lead Paint

Many house paints made before 1978 contain lead, which is a threat to children and can cause permanent brain damage, behavioral problems, and other serious health problems. If you live in a pre-1978 home, obtain free information on testing and safety precautions and for guidelines on whether the paint should be left alone, covered, or removed at www.epa.gov/lead.

You can test existing paint for lead using a simple kit. Following instructions, scrape the surface; apply the activator; and wipe.

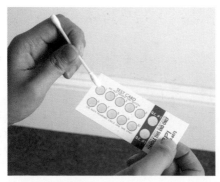

The activator makes a liquid sample on the swab that you then apply to the test card to find out the lead-content reading.

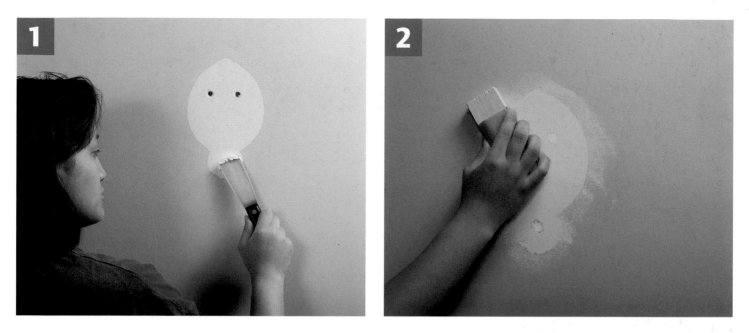

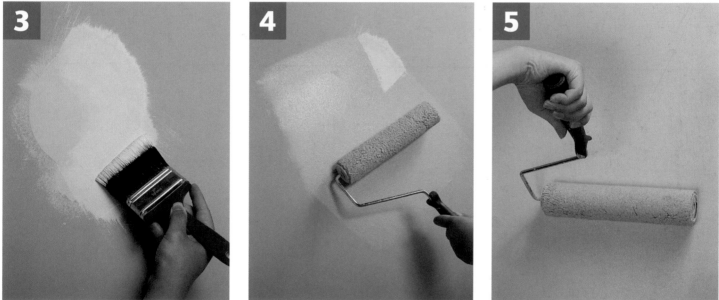

Sealing Over Stains

Remove surface stains as best as you can with a detergent/water solution or an appropriate solvent/ spot remover. To prevent remaining discoloration from bleeding through, seal the area with a stain-killing primer, such as pigmented white shellac. These sealers dry fast and won't slow you down. Similarly, coat knots in paneling or trim so that resins from the wood won't bleed through the final coat of paint.

Pigmented white shellac has tremendous hiding power. It also makes a good primer on metal.

Preparing Walls for Painting

Paint prep is a multistage process that has a direct bearing on the success of the paint job. The goal is to provide a smooth, clean surface for the new paint. In addition to making the repairs and covering stains, follow with these steps.

Prime Patches. If you don't treat the repairs you make, the paint will dry unevenly and ruin the job. Seal all repairs by applying a primer.

Clean the Area. Wipe down the walls to get rid of any sanding dust that may be there. Brush or vacuum along windowsills and the tops of baseboards.

Remove the Extras. Remove all of the switch and outlet covers. Tape the screws to the covers so that you will have them later. It also a good idea to remove all wall- and ceiling-mounted light fixtures. Remove as much furniture as possible, and cover everything else with drop cloths.

Basic Wall Prep

1 Scrape off any debris that may be on the walls, including any cracked or flaking paint. Flaking paint may be caused by a leak so it is a good idea to investigate the cause.

2 Some wall and ceiling damage inevitably tears the paper on the outside of the drywall. To stop a tear, cut the paper using a sharp utility knife.

3 Torn paper and other shallow surface damage are best repaired with two or three thin coats of drywall joint compound. Use a 12-in. flexible taping knife to spread the compound. Try to make the compound blend with the surrounding area, a process called "feathering." Sand lightly after each coat dries to provide the best surface for the next coat.

4 After the last coat of compound is dry, thoroughly sand every patch until it is smooth and even with the surrounding surfaces. To control the dust, use a palm sander with a dust collection system.

5 Spot prime all of the drywall repairs using latex primer. For areas that have stubborn stains, including watermarks, prime using a white-pigmented shellac. Move on to applying the topcoat of paint almost immediately.

tools and materials
◆ **Basic carpentry tools**
◆ **Utility knife**
◆ **Drywall joint compound**
◆ **Putty knives**
◆ **Fiberglass joint tape**
◆ **Masking tape**
◆ **Sandpaper or sander**
◆ **Power palm sander**
◆ **White shellac**

SMART TIP

Containing dust is a major concern when repairing walls. After the patching material is dry, try "sanding" it with a durable, damp sponge. This is a dustless method. Use 200-grit sandpaper only for the final sanding.

1

2

3

4

5

Filling Small Holes

1 Once a hole goes all the way through the drywall panel and is larger than 1½ to 1¾ inch in diameter, it won't hold the patching material you apply. Apply self-sticking fiberglass mesh tape over the hole, and press it firmly in place.

2 Spread a thin layer of joint compound over the damaged area. Wait for it to dry completely before applying a second coat.

1

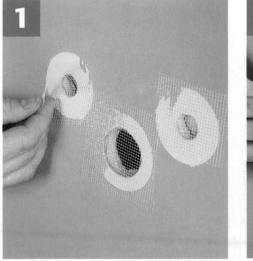

2

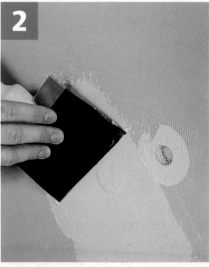

Dealing with Wallcoverings

Handling Old Wallcovering

tools and materials
- ◆ Scarifying tool
- ◆ Chemical stripper
- ◆ Roller and pad
- ◆ Drywall knife

1 In some cases, you can paint over old wallpaper as long as it is fully adhered. Cover with a primer first.

2 To remove paper, use a scarifying tool with wheels that chew through the paper.

3 To soften the wallcovering for scraping, apply chemical remover with a roller or use a steamer.

4 Scrape off the covering and glue using a drywall knife. You may need more than one application of remover.

Preparing Woodwork

The way to prepare wood trim for painting depends on the condition of the trim. If you are reusing old boards that have nicked or deeply scratched paint, you'll have to fill all holes and cracks with wood filler. Then sand the boards smooth so the filler won't be apparent when the boards are repainted, and clean up all the dust. If you are working on new boards, sand and apply a primer before painting.

Caulk all the joints between the trim boards and the walls and ceilings. Use paintable latex caulk.

On new wood, apply a primer. Use smooth brush strokes to achieve the best surface. Sand lightly.

SMART TIP

Rather than carry a heavy paint can around the room while working, pour a small amount of paint into a plastic paint bucket and work from that.

Painting Tools...3 Ways to Apply Paint

brush checklist
◆ Use nylon bristles for latex paint.
◆ Use natural bristles for oil-based paint.
◆ The tips of the bristles should be tapered and split for maximum control.

roller checklist
◆ Use a fine-napped sleeve to leave a smooth finish.
◆ Use a thick-napped roller to leave a pronounced stipple.
◆ Use 9-in. rollers on large walls; 3- or 4-in. rollers on small areas.

sprayer checklist
◆ Strain paint through cheesecloth to prevent lumps from clogging the spray tip.
◆ Always wear safety goggles and a respirator mask when spraying paint.

Painting Walls

Paint in this order: ceiling, walls, woodwork. If the ceiling and walls will be a different color, don't worry about the wall/ceiling juncture when painting the ceiling. You'll find it easier to overlap the boundary, and then cover your mistakes when you are painting the walls.

tools and materials

- ◆ Drop cloths and work lamp
- ◆ Screwdriver
- ◆ Paint and trim brush
- ◆ Paint roller and extension pole
- ◆ Roller pad and paint pan

Painting Woodwork

To get a clean job, remove any knobs from doors and cabinets before painting. Unless you need to paint large surfaces, use a small sash brush (1½ to 2 inches wide) to paint all wood. Paint the edges of doors first, ending with the larger surfaces. Use a paint shield while painting baseboards.

When painting a window sash, allow the paint to cover about ¹⁄₁₆ inch of glass to help seal the juncture between the glazing and the wood. Go back after the paint dries, and scrape any spills off of the glass using a razor blade.

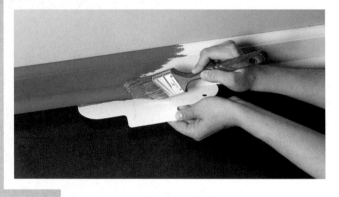

1 Save yourself cleanup time and effort by covering the work area with disposable drop cloths.

2 Remove cover plates on electrical switches and receptacles, as well as wall- and ceiling-mounted light fixtures.

3 A 2½-in. flagged and tipped sash brush works well to cut-in around trim and where the walls and ceiling meet.

4 Load up the roller evenly with paint. Use either a deep and sturdy pan or a 5-gal. bucket with a roller screen.

5 Apply a vertical swath of paint working from high to low. You'll spread out this heavy strip later.

6 Apply a second swath with a heavily loaded roller from low to high, a foot or so away from the first strip.

7 Spread the heavily coated strips by cross-rolling. This step should cover the entire working area with paint.

8 Use a moderately loaded roller (with an extension pole if needed) to finish coating the wall.

9 Remove lines at the end of strokes by applying less pressure and lifting the roller off the wall.

Paint and Primer Choices

PAINT	APPLICATIONS	PROS/CONS
Latex primer	New plaster or drywall, uncoated wallpaper, finished wood, new brick	Easy clean-up, quick-drying, almost odor-free; doesn't perform well on unfinished wood
Alkyd primer	New plaster or drywall, finished or unfinished wood, any new masonry	Best primer for wood, good for all paints; doesn't perform well on drywall, needs solvents for cleanup
Primer-sealer	Unfinished wood, mildew stains	Quick-drying, good for bleeding knots; needs alcohol for cleanup
Latex paint	Plaster/drywall, primed wood, vinyl trim, steel, aluminum, cast iron	Easy clean-up, quick-drying, inexpensive; not as strong as alkyd, needs primer over wood, adheres poorly to gloss finishes
Alkyd paint	Plaster/drywall, unprimed wood, vinyl trim, steel, aluminum, cast iron	More durable than latex, adheres to all types of paints; slow-drying, cleans up with solvents, needs primer for drywall and plaster

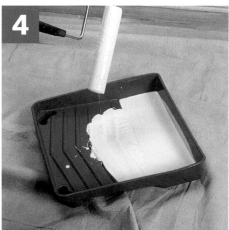

SMART TIP

Plan the job so that you complete large
sections at one time, pausing where there
is a natural break—for example, along the
edge of a window or door opening,
or at the edge of a wall.

Finishing Trimwork

tools and materials

- ◆ Scrapers and putty knife ◆ Sandpaper and block
- ◆ Crevice tool ◆ Heat gun (or chemical stripper)
- ◆ Sandpaper and block ◆ Brush and finish

1 Use a draw-scraper with a sharp blade to remove layers of paint. You can also use chemical stripper.

2 A heat gun can loosen paint enough for you to peel up layers using a putty knife. Don't let the paint bubble.

3 Crevice tools such as this one with a triangular shape are good for clearing paint from intricate molding.

4 You'll need to do some sanding to smooth the wood and remove paint embedded in the surface.

5 Wipe the trim with a tack rag to remove sanding dust, and paint, seal, or stain the wood to suit.

SMART TIP

In an older house it's smart to check for lead-based paint with a swab test before heating or scraping.

Refinishing Wood Trim

You can protect wood trim with a variety of clear finishes once you have stripped and sanded it smooth. Some, such as linseed oil, have only one ingredient while others include stain and sealer. Some are designed for a single, quick application, while others have long drying times and require multiple applications. (Some may be toxic and flammable, so always follow the manufacturer's instructions for safe application.)

◆ **Fast-Drying Finishes.** Coatings such as shellac and lacquer combine a small amount of solids with a large amount of thinner, which spreads the coating, evaporates, and leaves the solids to protect the wood. The drawback is that these finishes are difficult to apply properly.

◆ **Slow-Drying Finishes.** These coatings have more solids and less thinner. Finishes such as boiled linseed oil dry tacky and gradually harden.

◆ **Polyurethane Finishes.** To clear-finish trim, most people use polyurethane, which dries more slowly than shellac but provides a durable scratch- and moisture-resistant surface. Polyurethane is easy to apply using a brush. The finish is available in high- and low-gloss sheens, in oil- and water-based formulations. Is is a good choice for floor trim and other surfaces subject to wear and tear and wetness.

Applying Wallcoverings

Papering Outside Corners

For wrapping outside corners, follow the same procedure you used for the inside corners, opposite, but add ½ inch to the measurement. Place the paper in position, but before wrapping it around the corner, make small slits in the waste portions of the paper near the ceiling and the baseboard so you can turn the corner without wrinkling the paper.

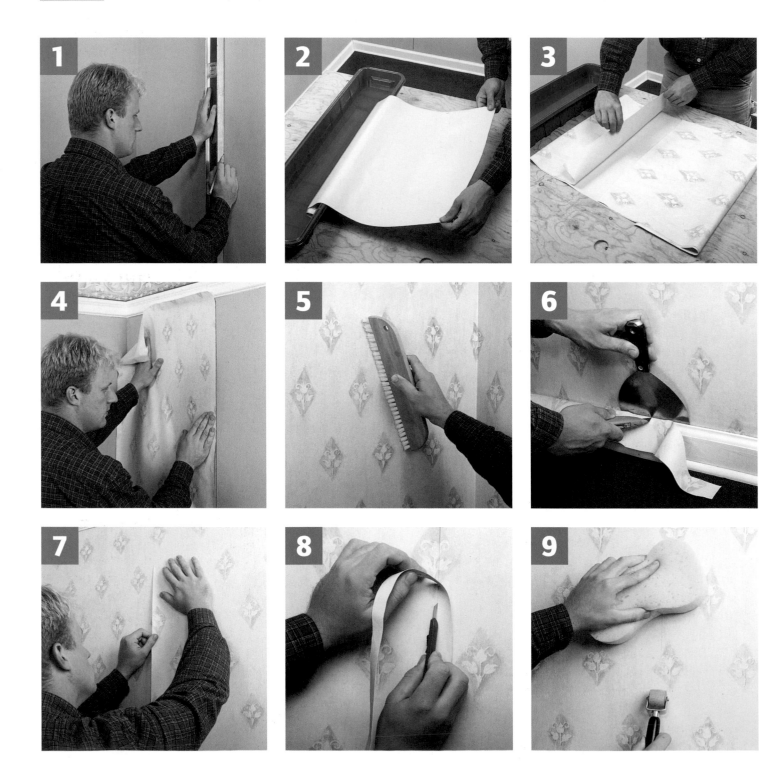

tools and materials

- ◆ 4-ft. level ◆ Tape measure ◆ Scissors
- ◆ Utility knife with extra blades ◆ Wallpaper trough
- ◆ 6-in. taping knife ◆ Smoothing brush ◆ Sponge
- ◆ Seam roller ◆ Seam adhesive ◆ Prepasted wallpaper
- ◆ Long straightedge

1 Use a 4-ft. level to mark a starting line on the wall. Draw the line from the floor to the ceiling.

2 Cut a piece of prepasted paper to length; then roll it up loosely; and lower it into a tub of lukewarm water. Slowly remove the paper.

3 Fold the wet paper onto itself from both directions. This is called booking the paper and makes it easier to carry.

4 Align the strip with the plumb line that is drawn on the wall. Start the strip slightly away from the line, and gently push it over to the line.

5 Use a smoothing brush to remove any air bubbles from under the paper. Work from the center toward the edges.

6 Trim the strip to length by first pressing a taping knife against the wall to create a sharp crease. Then cut along the edge of the knife using a sharp utility knife.

7 Hang the next strip on the wall.

8 On pieces that overlap, use a sharp knife to cut through both strips at once. Discard the cut pieces. Cutting both pieces like this creates a perfect seam.

9 Roll the cut seams flat using a wallpaper roller. Use a damp sponge to wipe away any paste or adhesive.

Papering Inside Corners

1 Measure to the edge of the last full sheet into the corner at the top, middle, and, bottom of the wall. Cut the paper ⅛-in. wider than the widest measurement.

2 Hang the cut piece, and smooth it into place using a wallpaper brush. This piece should turn the corner slightly.

3 Draw a plumb line on the second wall that matches the width of the waste piece left when the first sheet was cut. Align this piece with the plumb line, and smooth it in place.

4

Repairs and Maintenance

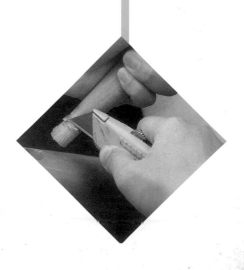

Repairing Windows

When the glass in old single-pane windows breaks or cracks, you can repair the windows with a new sheet of glass that you can get cut to size at the hardware store or home center. Hold the glass in place using glazing compound. Though glazing may look like it is an Old-World skill—such as thatching roofs or blacksmithing—it's really quite easy to master. The key is a clean surface and sustained pressure during the glazing application. It's not just good looks you are after. Tight windows reduce noise, as well as heating and cooling costs.

SMART TIP

Ready to upgrade from those old, drafty windows to energy-efficient units? Go to www.eere.energy.gov/consumer/ to get information on the windows that are right for your home.

Replacing Glass

tools and materials

◆ Putty knife ◆ Paintbrush
◆ Glass cutter (if needed) ◆ Primer
◆ New glass ◆ Eye protection
◆ Work gloves ◆ Glazier's points
◆ Glazing compound (See opposite.)

1 On an older window, the exterior putty may pop off the glass and frame easily when you scrape it with a putty knife.

2 Once the glass is out of the frame, scrape the wood underneath.

3 Prime raw wood where new compound will rest. This keeps moisture from seeping into the wood and weakening the bond.

4 Roll out a rope of fresh compound to back up the glass; set it against the sash; and press it in place with your fingers.

5 To secure the glass, set small holders, called glazier's points. Use a putty knife to force the points into the sash.

6 The exterior layer of compound covers the points. Smooth this layer using a putty knife, and use the edge to trim any excess.

Freeing a Stuck Sash

On older windows, particularly those that are not regularly opened, layers of paint can seal the sash in its track. Instead of forcing the sash or prying at the base and damaging the wood, release the painted-on seal. You can slice along the seam with a utility knife, making repeated passes to cut through the paint. A circular cutting wheel also works well and is easier to keep in the seam. Try working a putty knife with a thin, flexible blade along the seam. Sometimes the only permanent solution is to pry off the stop, and remove the window for a thorough scraping and sanding.

To free a sash stuck in place by many coats of paint, use a utility knife to make several scoring cuts between sash and stop.

A wheel cutter rides along the seam between the sash and the stop. You may also need to cut the paint film outside.

Glazing Compounds

At seams between dissimilar materials, such as glass and wood, which expand and contract at different rates, you need glazing compound. To form the compound, work it in your hands or roll it out on a board. If you need to make a glass repair in cold weather, first prepare the compound inside so that it's pliable when you work it along the window. The wood against which the compound rests should be primed. Otherwise, the compound can dry prematurely and crack. Follow the directions on the can. Once the compound dries, you will need to prime and paint it.

Traditional compound is an oily putty. You need to work it smooth until it's soft like dough, form a ball, and roll the ball into strips.

Preformed compound is available in plastic-backed strips. Peel the backing, and push the strip of compound in place.

Repairing Screens

You can fix a damaged screen more easily that you can replace a screen, but repairs are unsightly and about as fashionable as iron-on patches for your blue jeans. The best solution is to replace the entire screen. Unfortunately, working with screening can be frustrating and often requires the patience of a Zen monk. The work is not difficult, but unless you are careful, it is easy to end up with sagging screens that are not held tightly in the frame. Or you may end up with the grid out of alignment. But careful attention to detail usually produces good results. There are two ways to replace screens. The method shown below is for screens that are stapled to a wooden frame—a common situation on old screen doors. Opposite is a method that uses special screen frames that are available at most home centers.

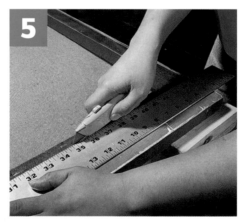

Replacing Screens

tools and materials

- ◆ Small pry bar
- ◆ Pliers ◆ Screwdriver
- ◆ C-clamps ◆ Staple gun
- ◆ Utility knife
- ◆ Straightedge
- ◆ Hammer ◆ Blocking
- ◆ New screening
- ◆ Staples
- ◆ Finishing nails

1 To replace damaged screens on a wood frame, start by prying off the trim pieces that hold the screen edges.

2 Use pliers and a screwdriver to pull the old staples and to remove the old screen. You may want to sand and paint the frame, too.

3 Use clamps to create a downward bow in the center of the frame. When you release the clamps at the end of the job, the screen tightens.

4 Spread a new piece of screen over the bowed frame, and staple it in place, starting at the center and working out.

5 Use a utility knife and a straightedge to trim away excess screen. You have to staple in a straight line to get a neat edge.

6 Finally, nail down the trim pieces that help to hold the screen tight and cover the rows of staples.

Screening Frames

Use shears or a utility knife to cut new screening with a 2-inch over-age on all sides. Lay it over the frame, and roll the screening into the channel with the wheel of a screen roller. Then roll the spline into the channel to tighten and hold the screen in place. Keep the screen tight as you work. With fiberglass or metal screens, it works best to install opposite sides in order.

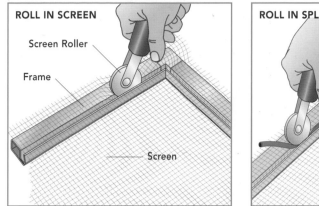

ROLL IN SCREEN

Screen Roller

Frame

Screen

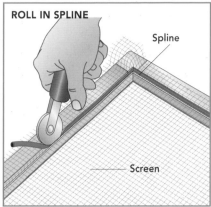

ROLL IN SPLINE

Spline

Screen

SMART TIP

Think all screens are the same? Think again. When it comes time to replace a screen on a window or door, you have a choice among a number of different screening materials. The most common type of screening is made of fiberglass and is available in charcoal, gray, and green colors. Aluminum screen resists sagging and corrosion, and can withstand harsh climates. Special solar screening, which is black, blocks much of the harmful rays of the sun while still providing visibility.

Maintaining Heating Systems

Heating systems combine electricity and combustible fuel — two of the most dangerous elements in your home. The electricity triggers a pilot that ignites gas or oil. Electrical power may also circulate hot air or water through your home by means of pumps and fans. Your heating system is really a small power plant that is hardwired to your home's electrical system and plumbed to an essentially limitless source of fuel—especially if you have natural gas service. Because there is no way for the fuel source to "know" how much fuel it should deliver, it just pipes in all that is consumed, whether you are taking the chill off of the house early in the spring or making the house warm and cozy in the dead of winter. So play it safe when it comes to heating systems. It is not worth the risk to your safety to try and save a few hundred dollars on furnace repair if you don't know exactly what you are doing. That's why this chapter recommends practices for maintaining and cleaning fans, heating units and ducts, and changing filters—easy, basic stuff that anyone can do and all homeowners should undertake to keep their systems running efficiently. Leave the work on power and gas features to trained experts.

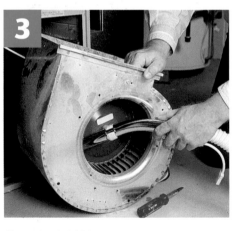

Cleaning Furnaces

tools and materials
- Screwdriver ◆ Vacuum
- Bucket or watering can
- Replacement dust filter
- Lubricating oil ◆ Disinfectant

1 Furnaces have air-intake grilles that are easily removed. Turn off the power supply first, and follow manufacturer's directions.

2 The most basic job, and one of the easiest, is to replace the dust filter. You may need to do this several times a year.

3 Use the small brush on a vacuum to clean the furnace blower. Removing the blower can make complete servicing easier.

4 For smooth and quiet operation, oil the blower motor (typically only 3 drops) according to manufacturer's directions.

5 On modern high-efficiency furnaces that produce condensation, clean the drain tube using a disinfecting solution.

SMART TIP

A furnace can receive power at multiple places, such as the blower unit and the electronic pilot system. Before working on your furnace, turn off the power to the unit, being mindful of the fact that it may be on two (or more) circuits.

Improving Efficiency

Some systems warm living spaces by transferring heat contained in water through hydronic baseboards and radiators. Anything that frustrates the efficient transfer of that heat (such as dust and dirt) reduces the efficiency of your heating system, which costs you money. Keep radiators and baseboards clean at all times.

Maximize heat from radiator and convectors by bleeding off trapped air. Do this by opening bleeder valves until the water flows.

In single-pipe systems, prevent cool water (or condensed steam) from blocking the inlet by raising the far end of the radiator.

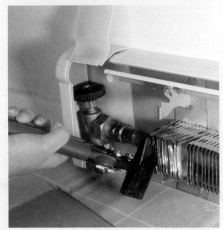

Increase the output of convectors by separating and aligning bent fin plates using pliers or a fin comb.

Cleaning Ducts

It is widely debated whether cleaning deep into the ducts is good practice. Some experts feel it stirs up more dust than it removes, and that dust eventually makes its way into the living area. But cleaning around registers and grills is widely recommended, and it can be accomplished using a household vacuum cleaner.

If your ducts have never been cleaned—even if you use furnace filters—remove a register, and check the duct walls inside.

A household vacuum may reach several feet down most ducts. A professional cleaning covers the entire duct system.

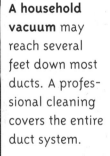

Dust that gets past your filters may eventually be trapped at the return-air grille, which also should be vacuumed.

Maintaining Central Air

The life of a central air-conditioning unit can be shortened if it is not cleaned regularly before the start of each cooling season. In warm-weather climates, air conditioners should be serviced several times a year. If you want to experience what it's like to be a dirty central air-conditioning unit, try to draw air through a straw. No problem, right? Now, what happens when you place two layers of tissue across the end of the straw? Obviously, it becomes more difficult to draw the air through. A dirty filter affects the air conditioner in the same way. Grimy, clogged filters make the compressor—the really expensive part of the air conditioner—work harder. The compressor's life is shortened, and you pay for the extra electricity required to operate the dirty unit. Let the air flow freely by changing the filter. It will only take a couple of minutes. If you have a manual, check it for specific instructions. If you don't, you can still clean around the grilles of the cabinet, the blades of the fan, the fan chassis, and the coil fins. However, central air-conditioning units require professional service for recharging refrigerant.

SMART TIP

On split system air conditioners, cold refrigerant is piped to an air exchanger. The insulation (black foam) that protects the pipe can get easily beat up, so repair or replace it, because an uninsulated pipe can drive down the unit efficiency.

Electronic Cleaners

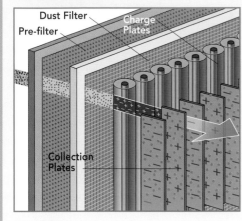

Electronic air filters are built into the ducts near your furnace. (A unit can be added to existing systems by modifying the ducts.) A typical electronic cleaner has a prefilter that is similar to a standard furnace filter. It traps large dust particles and can be removed for cleaning. Next in line is one or two metal boxes (also removable for cleaning) containing thin metal plates. Particles in the airflow, typically in the return duct, are positively charged on their way to the plates. The plates themselves are negatively charged to attract the particles, which are driven against the plate walls as they pass through the system. These appliances can remove over 90 percent of most airborne pollutants, including pollen and smoke particles. The drawback is that larger particles hitting the plates can make an annoying sound—like an outdoor bug-zapper. Be sure to keep the area around the filters clear, so air can flow into them in an unrestricted way.

Basic Cleaning

tools and materials

◆ Screwdriver
◆ Soft brush
◆ Fin comb
◆ Lubricating oil
◆ New air filter

1 The first step is to shut off power to the unit. Most systems have a cutoff box mounted outside near the fan unit. Check the product manual for instructions.

2 Remove the access panel, and use a garden hose and brush to clear any debris or grass clippings from cabinet grilles.

3 Clean the fan blades and fan motor housing, and lubricate the motor with oil as required by the manufacturer.

4 Use a soft brush to clear dust from coil fins. If some are bent, use a straightening tool or a fin comb to align them.

5 One of the easiest steps, but one of the most important, is to change air filters that keep dust out of the duct system.

Recharging

The refrigerant in older refrigerators, freezers, and air conditioners is typically an ozone-damaging hydrochlorofluorocarbon (HCFC) called Freon. Eventually, the closed refrigerant loop can develop a slow leak and cause the compressor to fail prematurely. It is illegal to release HCFCs into the atmosphere, so when an older machine needs repair, the service contractor is required to capture and recycle the refrigerant. Recycled HCFCs are used to recharge older machines. Most new models use less-damaging refrigerants, but you should still call in a pro to recharge even newer units.

Homeowners can take care of basic maintenance, but you need a contractor to recharge the refrigerant.

Sealing Surfaces

ike a child in a fairy tale who mistakenly obtains magic powers beyond his or her understanding, the first-time caulker often gets into more than they bargained for. The scenario goes like this: the caulker cuts open the tube, applies a little pressure, and uh oh, another force seems to take over. Far more caulk than the caulker needs or can manage flows from the tube. And, of course, the mess of uneven, hardened caulk is in a spot for everyone to see. Actually, caulking is easy, but it takes practice. The trick is to cut a small hole in the tip of the tub, and when using a caulking gun, release the pressure on the cartridge by pressing the tab on the handle when you want the flow to stop.

Applying Latex Caulk

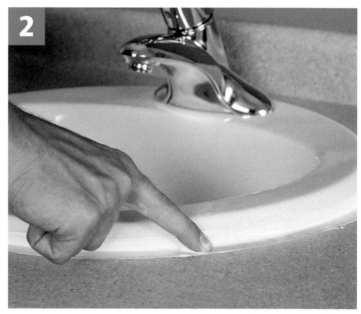

tools and materials

◆ **New sink**
◆ **Countertop**
◆ **Pencil**
◆ **Tub-and-tile caulk**
◆ **Saber saw**
◆ **Sponge**

1 To seal between the sink and countertop, apply a bead of latex tub-and-tile caulk around the basin's rim.

2 Use a finger to force the caulk under the basin's rim. There's no need to take great pains to be neat.

3 Use a wet sponge to smooth the joint and remove excess caulk. Leave only a thin line of caulk behind.

SMART TIP

Confused about which caulk to use? The chart opposite explains characteristics of some of the common caulks. Manufacturers make it easy to choose caulk by displaying on the tube where the products should be used.

Sealing Tile Grout

Seal grout between glazed ceramic tiles from moisture and staining by brushing on a grout sealer. Ceramic floor tiles can be glazed or unglazed. The unglazed type, shown far right, is a common choice for both bathrooms and kitchens. To protect them from staining, apply a sealer every year or two. A medium-nap roller ("nap" is the furry part of the roller, and a medium-nap roller is one that is not too furry and not too flat) is ideal for applying sealer. Note that sealer can be very sloppy, so approach wall areas slowly.

To protect grout joints—the weak links in a tile floor—you can take the extra step of applying a sealer to the grout only.

Seal unglazed tiles and grout with a transparent sealer. Roll diagonally to cover the tile and force the sealer into the grout lines.

Common Caulks

Acrylic Latex
Slightly longer-lasting than similar, cheaper vinyl latex, acrylic latex is inexpensive and easy to apply, but degrades in direct sunlight and adheres poorly to porous surfaces.
◆ **Drying skin: ½ hour** ◆ **Curing: 1 week** ◆ **Life: 5–10 years**

Butyl
Also called butyl rubber, this caulk has better adhesion and stretching ability than acrylic, but costs more and takes longer to cure. It also degrades in sunlight.
◆ **Drying skin: 24 hours** ◆ **Curing: 6 months** ◆ **Life: 5–10 years**

Polyurethane
Polyurethane caulks are expensive and more difficult to apply than latex and butyl, but they last longer, can cover a wider gap (up to ¾ inch), and will stretch further.
◆ **Drying skin: 24 hours** ◆ **Curing: 1 month** ◆ **Life: 20+ years**

Silicone
Not to be confused with paintable siliconized acrylic—silicone has good stretching ability and can cover a 1-inch gap, but it can't be painted and adheres poorly to plastic and wood.
◆ **Drying skin: 1 hour** ◆ **Curing: 1 week** ◆ **Life: 20+ years**

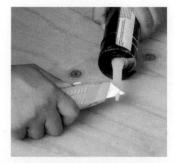

Use a utility knife to trim an angled opening in the cartridge tip.

To keep adhesive from hardening in the tip between jobs, insert a common nail.

Repairing Damaged Floors

There is a certain feeling of doom and finality that homeowners experience when a sharp object they have dropped punctures a vinyl floor. Or when Rover, left alone for too long, stains a new $5,000 carpet or shiny hardwood floor. The sense of doom is not necessary. Nearly any floor — vinyl, wood, tile, carpet — can be fixed with a patch. How evident the patch will be in the repaired floor depends only on your skill in sizing and cutting the patch, or in matching the color of the stain and finish. Practice on some scrap material first. You will be surprised at the boost to your self-confidence when you master the technique. These tasks can be completed using common tools available at most home centers.

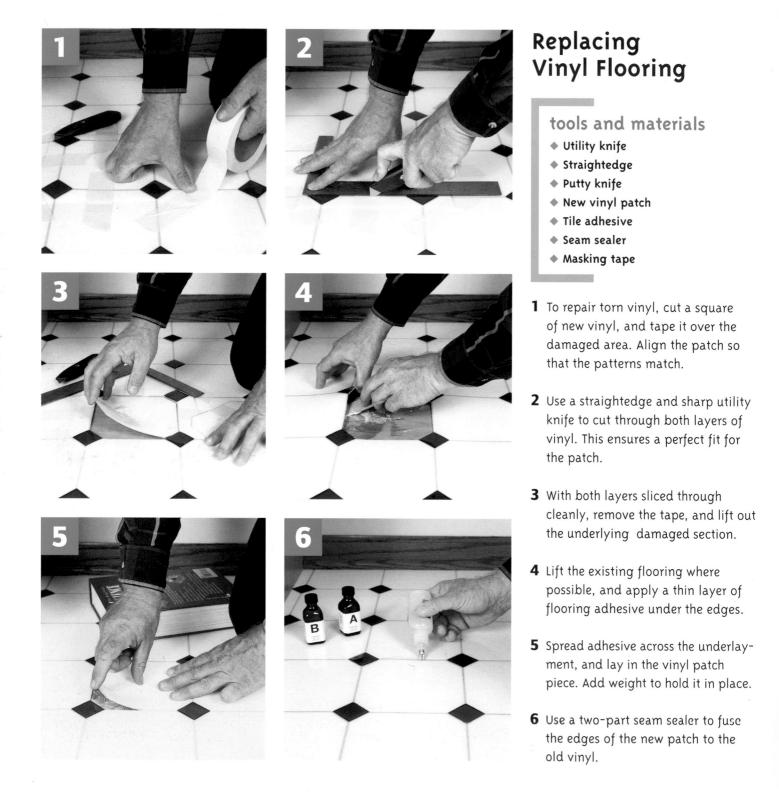

Replacing Vinyl Flooring

tools and materials

- ◆ Utility knife
- ◆ Straightedge
- ◆ Putty knife
- ◆ New vinyl patch
- ◆ Tile adhesive
- ◆ Seam sealer
- ◆ Masking tape

1 To repair torn vinyl, cut a square of new vinyl, and tape it over the damaged area. Align the patch so that the patterns match.

2 Use a straightedge and sharp utility knife to cut through both layers of vinyl. This ensures a perfect fit for the patch.

3 With both layers sliced through cleanly, remove the tape, and lift out the underlying damaged section.

4 Lift the existing flooring where possible, and apply a thin layer of flooring adhesive under the edges.

5 Spread adhesive across the underlayment, and lay in the vinyl patch piece. Add weight to hold it in place.

6 Use a two-part seam sealer to fuse the edges of the new patch to the old vinyl.

Removing Stains from Wood Floors

If you have an area that has been stained by a pet, you can remove both the stain and odor using wood bleach or household bleach after sanding the area down to bare wood. Soak the sanded area with full-strength bleach; let the wood dry; sand again; and soak the wood a second time. Because bleach kills odors but also lightens the wood, stain the patch before resealing the surface. Apply several coats of polyurethane to seal any odors in the wood, and blend the surface with coats of wax.

There are dozens of recipes for removing stains, but one of the oldest and most reliable is household bleach.

Once a dark stain is lightened, sand lightly, and then blend the repair using stain and paste wax.

Spot Patching Carpets

1 Obtain a carpet repair kit. Use a circular carpet patch tool to remove a cookie-cutter section around a deep stain, burn, or tear.

2 Peel the cover tape from a piece of double-faced adhesive patch tape. Cut it larger than the hole, and fold to insert.

3 Use the circular cutter to cut a patch piece from a remnant, and press it firmly in place.

Unsticking Cabinet Doors and Drawers

During a realtors apprenticeship, master realtors must instruct their protégés in selling phrases such as this one delivered during tours of old kitchens, "The cabinets stick a little, but that's easy to fix." This is usually delivered with a dismissive hand gesture. Many of us are lulled into acceptance by that wave of the hand. Because at cabinet repair time, many mere mortals stand baffled in front of sagging doors that need to be squared or drawers that stick every time you try to open them. The repairs, it seems to many, will require ancient carpentry techniques and arcane tools. Well, the techniques aren't so ancient and the tools are more commonplace than arcane. Dive in. Smoothly operating door and drawers are well worth the effort.

If the Door Sticks on the Latch Side

Half the battle is knowing exactly where the door sticks. Find out by coating the edge with powdered chalk.

Start planing where chalk has rubbed off on the cabinet, and gradually work away from the high spot.

If the Door Sticks on the Hinge Side

If the door has a gap near the top, remove the hinge, and make a cardboard filler to build out the mortise.

If the door is too tight near the top, remove the door, and use a chisel to slightly deepen the hinge mortise.

Unsticking Drawers

Sometimes lubricating the cleats and runners does the trick—try running a bar of soap or a candle over them.

If lubrication doesn't work, you can plane or sand the runners slightly, test-fitting the drawer as you go.

Fixing Bowed Bottoms

Remove nails on bottom or corners. If necessary, separate corner joints; remove the bottom; and re-glue the sides square.

Slide the drawer bottom back into its slot, but don't glue in place. Drawers can be cut low in back for bottom repairs.

SMART TIP

Use a larger screw, if possible, in a worn screw hole. Otherwise, wood filler or a wooden dowel (or a toothpick or two) can be trimmed and dipped in glue to fit snugly into a worn screw hole. The idea is to provide fresh material into which screws can bite.

Cabinet hardware is designed to support only limited loads; it can easily be overstressed if doors are ill-fitting. You can improve holding capacity by filling in the existing holes and giving the screw threads solid material to turn through. Use a paste-type wood filler, dowel, or several wooden toothpicks to fill the hole. Trim off the protruding ends, and drive in new screws with wide threads.

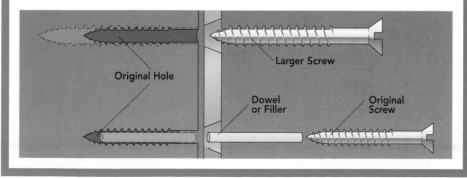

Original Hole

Larger Screw

Dowel or Filler

Original Screw

Fixing Locks

Most readers recognize that there is a reason that locks have metal chassis that conceal their inner workings and machinations: they are meant to remain secret and untouched by human hands. But even mechanisms assembled by mechanical masters are subject to failure, and if the failure happens to the lock on your front door, you need to jump into the breech when repairs are required. At worst, if your repairs fail, you can always rip the lock out entirely, smash it to bits with a hammer as just punishment, and replace the lock with a brand new one that works just fine. In fact, many locks in need of repair come back to life with some metal lubricant, or the removal of dirt or the occasional broken key shaft.

SMART TIP

INSTALLING LOCKS

Adding a deadbolt to an existing door involves drilling holes for the cylinder and bolt. But most of these products come with paper templates that show you exactly where to drill. If someone can break glass on or around the door and reach in to unlock the door, install a lock with a keyed inside cylinder. Just make sure you keep the key near the door and let your family know where it is in case of emergency.

Window Locks

Modern rotating window locks are designed for two purposes. First, they keep the window from being opened. Second, the rotating action of the lock draws the two window frames together to form a thermal seal that helps to keep out the cold and wind. They are not very costly, even the best ones, so spare no expense when shopping for new or replacement items. Most simply screw right to the window.

This rotating lever lock slides under the adjacent housing on the outer sash to join the two sections together.

This rotating cam lock is harder to pick from the outside because it clips around the housing on the outer sash.

This sash lock has a stub that travels in a slotted bracket. In this position, the stub is out of the way so the sash opens.

Keyed window locks are secure, but can be inconvenient if you need to find and use a key every time you want some ventilation.

This window lock increases security with a small stop that prevents the lock from turning unless you squeeze the handle.

Vacation Checklist

✔ **Don't close up**
Leave signs of normal activity, such as a rake on the front lawn.

✔ **Stop deliveries**
Don't let mail or newspapers accumulate while you're gone.

✔ **Phone calls**
Leave your answering machine on, and clear the messages from your vacation spot.

✔ **Outside lights**
Put outdoor lights on a timer, photoelectric switch, or motion-sensor switch.

✔ **Inside lights**
Mimic your normal schedule by putting upstairs and downstairs lights on automatic timers.

✔ **Trigger activity**
Put some indoor lights on special switches that turn on when they detect noise or motion—such as lamps near your front porch.

✔ **Fill the driveway**
If possible, ask a neighbor to park one of their cars in your driveway while you are away.

Fixing Common Lock Problems

Common lock problems include locks that have frozen mechanically because metal parts are stuck in place—easily treatable with a lubricant, such as WD40; locks that become jammed when moisture inside the lock freezes—these can be thawed using a hair dryer or volatile solvent such as alcohol; and locks where a key has broken off inside the lock—admittedly a difficult extraction that you can attempt using a sliver of sturdy metal.

When a lock sticks or is slow in responding, it may be clogged with dirt. Lubricate the cylinder with penetrating oil.

If you can't push in a key because of ice in the lock, thaw it out using a hair dryer, or heat the key using a match and work it in.

When a key breaks inside a lock, lift up the broken end using a narrow piece of metal, and remove the stub using pliers.

Repairing Wooden Furniture

Most readers will agree that there is something unsettling about sitting on a wobbly chair. That's a universal experience. But for many, that feeling is often compounded with dread because they are aware that they will soon be called upon to fix the problem—a daunting, baffling exercise that often requires visualizing the three-dimensional repaired chair when its parts are strewn about you on the floor. If you are not good at that sort of thing—and most of us aren't—document the chair disassembly process with drawings and photos, and label each piece. Fortunately, most repairs, such as the ones shown here, do not require taking the furniture apart. But even if you are faced with a more extensive repair, you have nothing to lose but an old piece of broken furniture if you fail, so dive in, and give it a try.

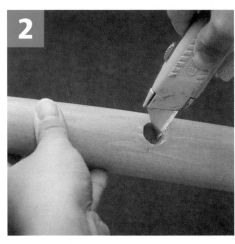

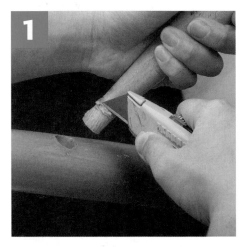

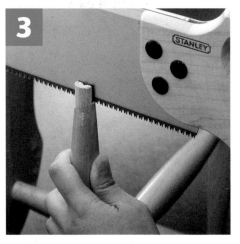

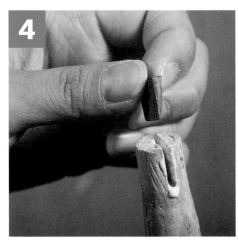

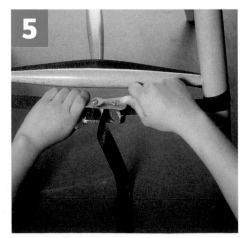

Repairing a Rung

tools and materials
- Utility knife
- Backsaw
- Band clamp
- Precut wedge
- Wood glue

1 Start by scraping off any old glue from the rung using a utility knife. This helps fresh glue adhere to the old surface.

2 Also scrape away old glue from the mortise. A power Dremel-type tool with a burr attachment is handy for this job.

3 Cut a slit, called a kerf, in the end of the rung using a backsaw. Before assembling the pieces, coat all mating surfaces with glue.

4 Cut a small, hardwood wedge that is about as long as the saw kerf. Start the wedge in the kerf before seating the rung.

5 Reassemble the chair after applying glue. A band clamp that ratchets tight is ideal for tightening several joints at once.

SMART TIP

Because the legs of chairs taper, it is difficult to use clamps to hold the legs together after they are glued. Straps and ropes will serve you well instead. Direct pressure on a joint is ideal, but indirect pressure may have to suffice. Use fast-drying glues.

Two Ways of Re-gluing

Add a Dowel

1a To strengthen a weak rung, check your alignment, and drill a hole through the chair leg into the center of the rung.

1b After injecting glue into the hole, gently hammer in a dowel until it seats. Cut off the dowel using a backsaw.

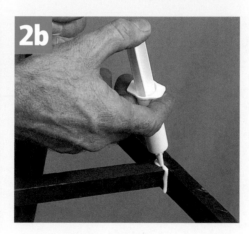

Re-glue a Tenon

2a To strengthen a weak tenon, drill a small hole at an angle into the joint through both mortise and tenon.

2b Insert the syringe tip into the hole, and inject a thinned-down polyvinyl glue. Wipe off the excess, and sand smooth.

Angle Drilling

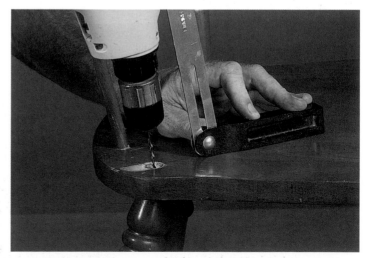

Because many joints between furniture components are at odd angles, you need to align the drill with mating parts.

To make sure that your angle is correct, set a bevel square to an existing component, and use it to guide your drill.

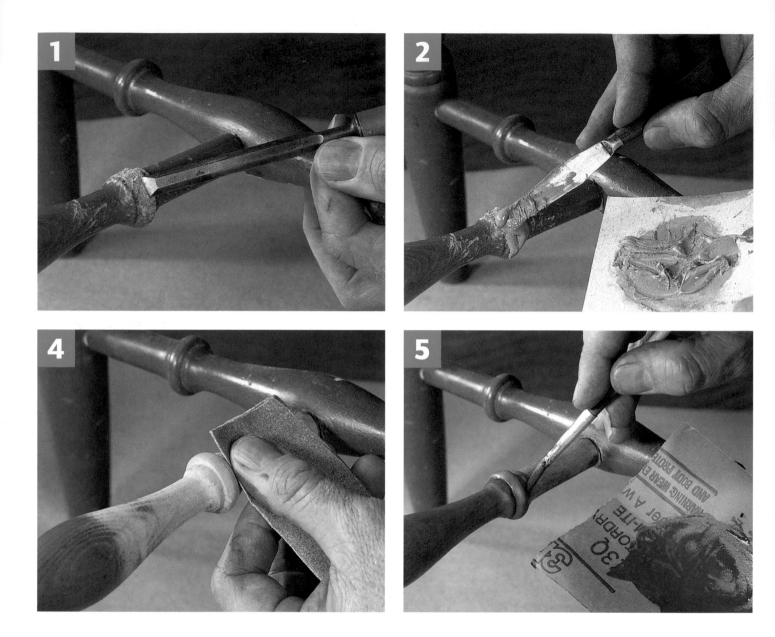

Fixing Moisture Stains

Use fine steel wool to rub over the stained area. Apply firm pressure in the direction of the grain.

Use fine wet-dry sandpaper to sand the area. It helps to use a small amount of mineral spirits as a lubricant.

Rub the area again using fine steel wool and paste wax. Finish by buffing with a soft cotton cloth.

3
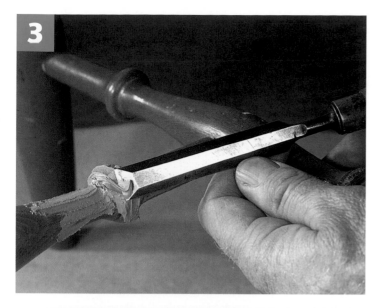

6

Repairing Wood Damage

tools and materials

- ◆ Wood chisel ◆ Brush
- ◆ Wood filler ◆ Dry stain
- ◆ Touch-up stain and finish
- ◆ Sandpaper

1 Use a wood chisel to cut off loose wood from the damaged area. Don't smooth it out—filler bonds best to a rough surface.

2 Mix the wood filler, and apply it to the damaged area. Add enough material to allow trimming and shaping later on.

3 When the filler is dry, use a small, sharp wood chisel to shape the filled area close to the desired shape.

4 Use sandpaper to trim and blend in the repaired section. Small, Dremel-type power tools have bits that make cutting and sculpturing jobs much easier.

5 Use a small brush to stain the repaired area. Match the color of the surrounding wood as closely as possible.

6 After the stain dries, apply as many coats of finish as necessary to blend with the surrounding finish.

Selecting the Right Sandpaper

Even with the best tools to cut and join wood, every project needs sandpaper for final smoothing and finishing.

DESCRIPTION/GRIT	PURPOSE AND COMMENTS
Extra coarse/12–36	Rough sanding, shaping; not recommended for furniture
Coarse/40–50	Rough sanding, shaping, paint removal, rarely used
Medium/60–80	Rough sanding to remove scratches; follow with finer grit
Fine/100–150	Preliminary sanding of wood before applying finish
Very fine/180–240	Pre-finish prep of hardwoods; between-coat sanding
Extra fine/280–320	Sanding and smoothing finishes between coats
Superfine/360–400	Sanding and smoothing finishes between coats
Ultrafine/500–600 and up	Sanding final finish coats, usually with water or oil

5
Plumbing Projects

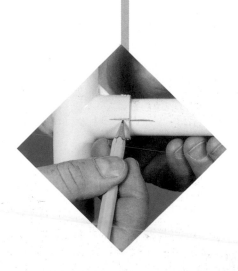

Fixing Compression Faucets

Compression faucets are the old-fashion kind that have rubber washers that control the flow of water. It is common for the washers to fail and the faucet to leak. If the faucet drips from the end of the spout, you'll have to replace the seat washers, and frequently, the seats themselves. Replacing a washer is easy (See below.) Before starting, buy a packet of washers so you will be sure to have the right size handy.

If the faucet leaks around its handles when the water is turned on but not when the water is shut off, the stem packing is worn. (See page 67.)

On most faucets, you will need to remove the stainless-steel or shiny metal shroud to get to the copper, brass, or steel nuts and fittings beneath. Anything shiny is usually decoration. Look for a screw that holds the cap in place.

SMART TIP

Crescent wrenches ("C wrenches") accumulate grime in their gears over time. So buy a new wrench, which will dramatically reduce slippage that can scuff your expensive fixtures.

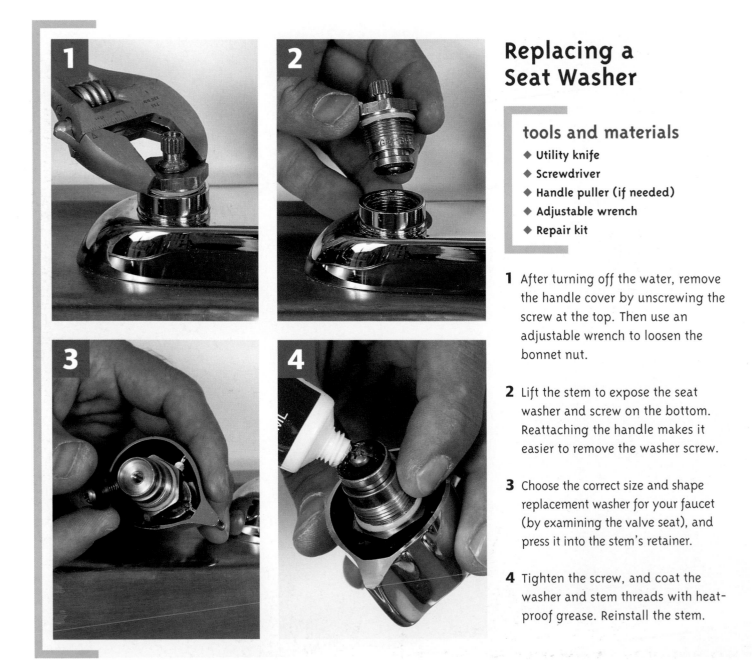

Replacing a Seat Washer

tools and materials
- ◆ Utility knife
- ◆ Screwdriver
- ◆ Handle puller (if needed)
- ◆ Adjustable wrench
- ◆ Repair kit

1 After turning off the water, remove the handle cover by unscrewing the screw at the top. Then use an adjustable wrench to loosen the bonnet nut.

2 Lift the stem to expose the seat washer and screw on the bottom. Reattaching the handle makes it easier to remove the washer screw.

3 Choose the correct size and shape replacement washer for your faucet (by examining the valve seat), and press it into the stem's retainer.

4 Tighten the screw, and coat the washer and stem threads with heat-proof grease. Reinstall the stem.

Repairing a Packing Washer

tools and materials

- ◆ Screwdriver
- ◆ Adjustable wrench
- ◆ Packing materials
- ◆ Pliers
- ◆ Handle Puller (if needed)

1 To repair a leak coming from the area of the packing washer, shut off the water, and remove the handle and bonnet nut.

2 Pry off the old graphite packing washer using a flat-blade screwdriver, and slide a new washer onto the stem.

3 Wrap packing string around the stem to finish the job. For a quick fix, you can instead add packing string to the packing in an old faucet.

SMART TIP

A handle puller is an inexpensive way to remove a stuck handle. Apply WD40 to the threads; attach the hook-like jaws of the handle puller; and crank down on the top to lift the handle.

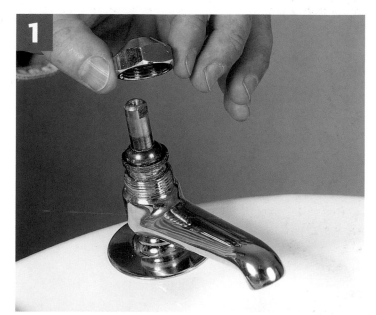

Fixing Washerless Faucets

I f you have taken even one philosophy class, you may already be asking this penetrating existential question: if washers wear out, why do faucets use them at all? The fact is, something has to seal the spaces between the faucet's moving metal parts because you can never get a metal-on-metal connection that's truly watertight. So "washerless" faucet is not really an accurate term because many of these rely on washers and the like to keep from dripping. The most popular types are ball-type, cartridge-type, and ceramic-disk faucets. (See below through page 73.)

Repairing Ball-Type Faucets

tools and materials
- Screwdriver
- Groove-joint pliers
- Allen wrench
- Ball-type faucet repair kit

SMART TIP

It's hard to tell the difference between old and new springs and seals, so throw out the old ones as soon as you remove them to avoid mixing them up.

1 To reach the handle screw, shut off the water, and tip back the handle. Insert an Allen wrench or faucet tool, and remove the screw.

2 Loosen the cam nut to gain access to the ball assembly. (See the exploded view of the faucet on the opposite page.) Delta faucets have slotted nuts (inset); Peerless units have surfaces that you can grasp using a wrench.

3 Lift the plastic cam to expose the ball assembly below. At the least, plan to replace the cam and the faucet seals.

4 Lift the ball from the faucet body, and set it aside. Some kits come with replacement balls and some do not, so choose accordingly.

5 Use an Allen wrench or thin screwdriver to lift the rubber seals and springs from the inlet and outlet openings. Replace them all.

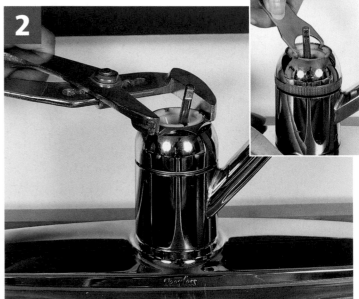

Cleaning an Aerator

Mineral-encrusted aerators are easy to unscrew from the faucet spout for cleaning or replacement.

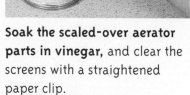

Soak the scaled-over aerator parts in vinegar, and clear the screens with a straightened paper clip.

Ball-Type Faucet Anatomy

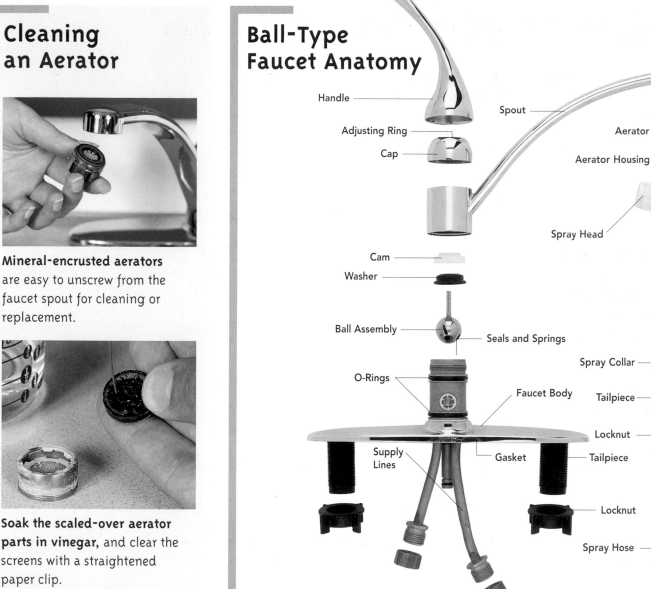

Handle

Spout

Aerator

Aerator Housing

Adjusting Ring

Cap

Spray Head

Cam

Washer

Ball Assembly

Seals and Springs

Spray Collar

O-Rings

Faucet Body

Tailpiece

Locknut

Supply Lines

Gasket

Tailpiece

Locknut

Spray Hose

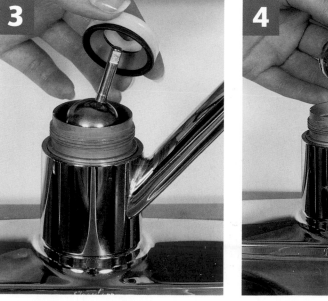

SMART TIP

Sometimes mineral buildup makes cartridges hard to remove from the faucet. Pour a little vinegar into the cavity, and wait a few minutes. The cartridge should break free when you next pull on it.

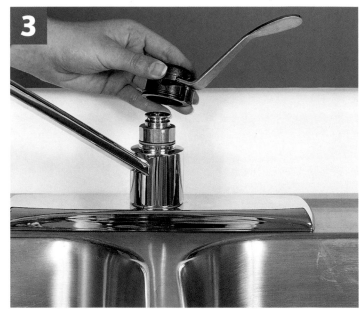

Repairing a Kitchen Cartridge Faucet

tools and materials

- ◆ Screwdriver
- ◆ Needle-nose pliers
- ◆ Adjustable wrench
- ◆ New cartridge

1 To get access to the handle screw, lift the decorative cap from the column. If there's no lift-off cap, pry up the index cap.

2 Remove the handle screw using a Phillips-head screwdriver. The screw is threaded into the stem of the cartridge.

3 Lift the handle and hood from the faucet to reveal the pivot nut. The hood covers the top of the cartridge.

4 Use an adjustable wrench to remove the pivot nut. Rotate the nut counterclockwise to unscrew it from the faucet body.

5 Using needle-nose pliers, withdraw the retainer clip to remove the cartridge (inset), and lift out the cartridge by the stem. Replace with a new cartridge.

Carriage Faucet Anatomy

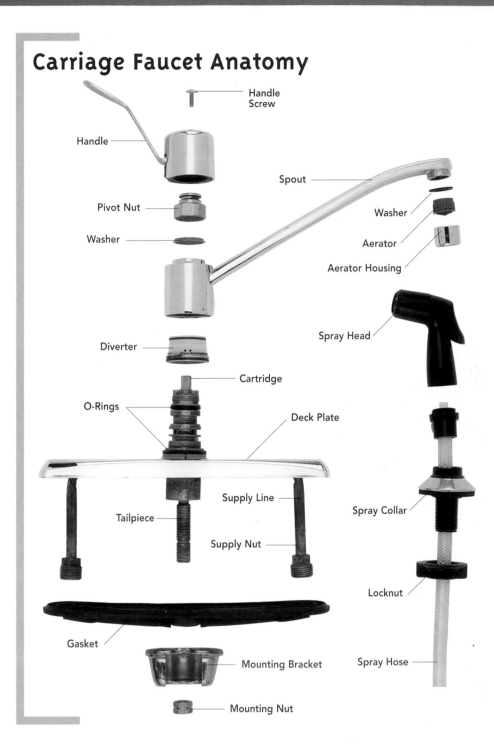

Handle Screw

Handle

Spout

Pivot Nut

Washer

Washer

Aerator

Aerator Housing

Spray Head

Diverter

Cartridge

O-Rings

Deck Plate

Supply Line

Tailpiece

Spray Collar

Supply Nut

Locknut

Gasket

Mounting Bracket

Spray Hose

Mounting Nut

Watch the Sleeve

Many single-handle cartridge faucets require an extra step before you can remove the retaining clip that holds the cartridge in place. With the handle off the faucet, look for a decorative stainless-steel sleeve (which keeps the clip from backing out) installed over the cartridge and column. Pull the sleeve from the column using your hands; remove the clip; and replace the cartridge. If you installed the cartridge incorrectly and the hot and cold are reversed, rotate the stem 180 degrees.

Fixing a Leak in a Ceramic-Disk Faucet

tools and materials

◆ Allen wrench
◆ Flat-blade screwdriver
◆ Groove-joint pliers
◆ New cartridge
◆ Tweezers

1 To locate the handle screw, shut off the water and tip the handle back. Use an Allen wrench to remove the screw.

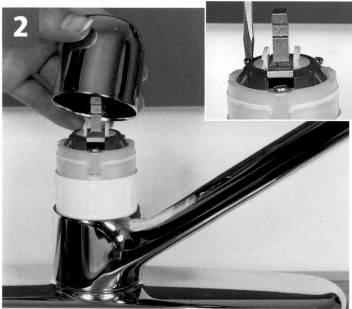

2 Lift off the decorative cap to expose the cartridge. Using a flat-blade screwdriver, loosen the screws at the top of the cartridge (inset).

3 Look for sediment near either or both of the inlet ports. Clear the sediment, and clean the seals—or replace the cartridge.

SMART TIP

Soak a mineral-hardened spray nozzle in warm vinegar to dissolve calcified minerals and enable it to work properly.

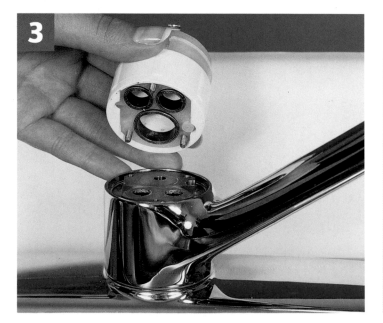

Don't Shatter the Ceramic

Ceramic disks are extremely durable, but they have one weakness. When you turn off the water at the shutoff valve and then open the faucet to get rid of that last bit of water before making the repair, you allow air into the pipes. When you turn the water back on, the water forces the air out of the pipes and through the faucet. This pressure can shatter the ceramic disk, resulting in a leaking faucet. To avoid this, open the shutoff valve slowly, allowing the air to escape gradually.

Ceramic-Disk Faucet Anatomy

SMART TIP

Sometimes you can refurbish a ceramic-disk cartridge by cleaning or replacing its neoprene seals, but more often you'll have to replace the entire cartridge.

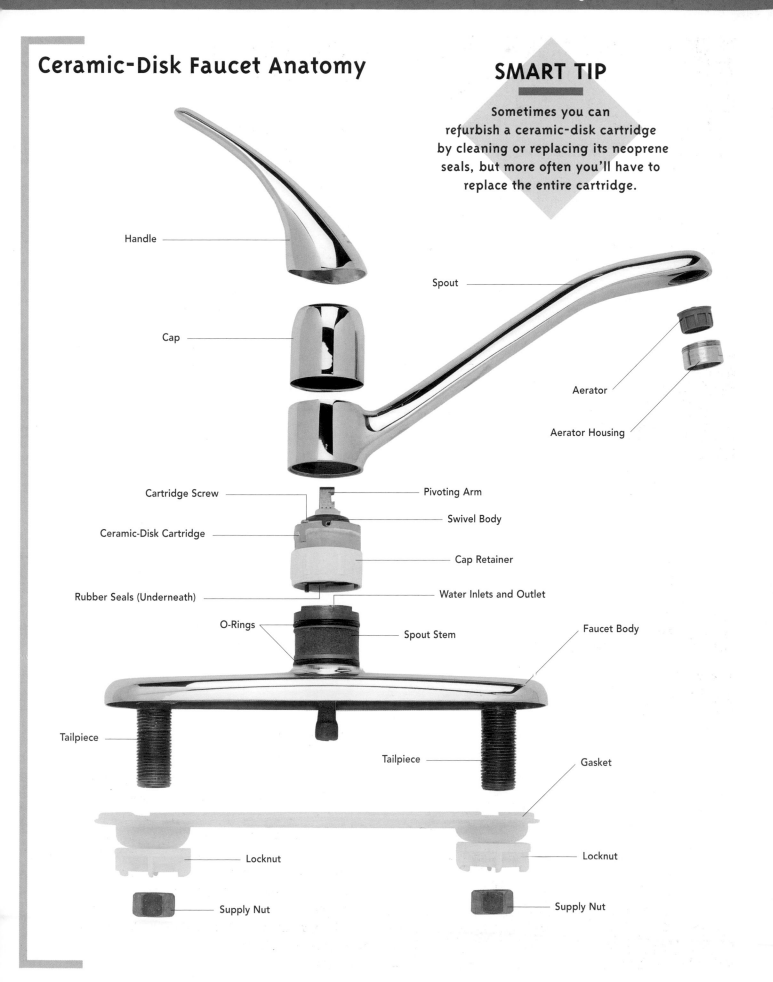

Handle

Spout

Cap

Aerator

Aerator Housing

Cartridge Screw

Pivoting Arm

Swivel Body

Ceramic-Disk Cartridge

Cap Retainer

Rubber Seals (Underneath)

Water Inlets and Outlet

O-Rings

Spout Stem

Faucet Body

Tailpiece

Tailpiece

Gasket

Locknut

Locknut

Supply Nut

Supply Nut

Installing a Faucet

nstalling a faucet isn't difficult, but it can be awkward. If you are replacing an existing faucet, you will need to lie on your back and reach up behind the sink to make the connections. There's a nifty gadget called a basin wrench that extends your reach, but it is still an uncomfortable working position. If you are installing a new sink at the same time, follow the sequence below and make most of the connections with the sink resting on the counter or some other work surface. Once the faucet is attached to the sink, connect the water supply tubes to the shutoff valves.

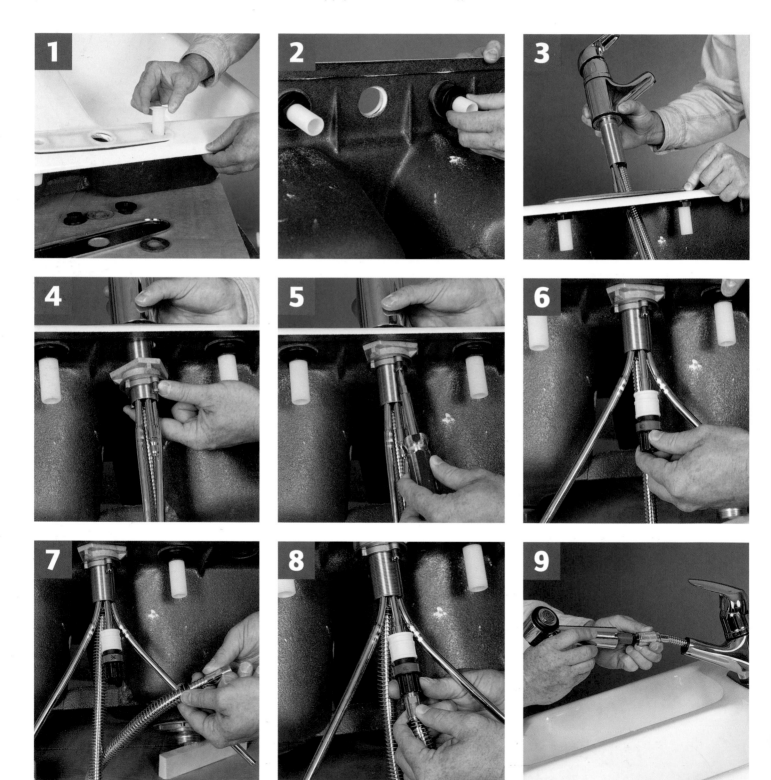

SMART TIP

To make sure a compression nut is really finger-tight, wiggle the supply tube while tightening.

Installing a New Faucet

tools and materials

- ◆ New faucet
- ◆ Screwdriver
- ◆ Groove-joint pliers
- ◆ Latex
- ◆ Tub-&-tile caulk

1 Center-column faucets work on sinks with one or three holes. For a multihole sink, install a base plate.

2 Fasten the plastic base-plate support/gasket from below using plastic jamb nuts. Make them finger-tight.

3 Snap the decorative base plate in place over the plastic support, and insert the faucet's column through the center hole.

4 Slide the mounting hardware onto the column and tighten it. The unit shown has a plastic spacer, steel washer, and brass nut.

5 Use a screwdriver to drive the setscrews against the large washer. Stop when the screws feel snug.

6 Install the supply adapter on the faucet nipple. Most faucets use a slip fitting with an O-ring seal, as shown.

7 Pull back the spiral tension spring at the bottom end of the spray hose to expose the male attachment threads.

8 Tighten the male threads into the bottom of the faucet's supply adapter. Stop when it feels snug. Don't overtighten.

9 From above, thread the outlet end of the hose into the spray head. Pull the hose out several times to test it for ease of use.

Attaching a Drain

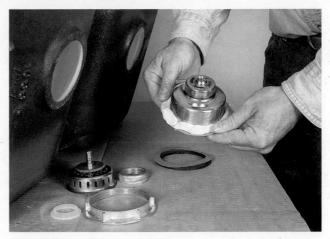

1 Form plumber's putty into a ½-in. roll several inches long, and press it against the underside of the drain flange.

2 Insert the drain through the sink opening, and install the rubber gasket, paper gasket, and spud nut in that order.

3 Use a spud wrench or large pliers to tighten the spud nut. Trim any excess putty from around the flange in the sink, and tighten the nut again.

Unclogging Drains

Few things are as inconvenient, or as disgusting, as a clogged drain. Of course, some clogs are worse than others. But all have one thing in common: the goal is to get rid of the clog so that the drain flows freely again. Some of the remedies shown here call for using a power auger—a good tool to rent when you need one. Here's a tip when using a plunger, always keep water in the sink, tub, or toilet. It helps maintain the plunger's seal and adds downward force against the clog.

1

Clearing a Tub Drain

tools and materials
◆ Screwdriver
◆ Drain auger
◆ Needle-nose pliers

2

1 Try the simple solutions first. Plug the overflow fitting with a wet rag, and use a plunger on the clog. Maintain a firm seal.

2 If the plunger does not work, remove the two overflow screws (inset), and pull out the mechanism—it's called a tripwaste. Insert the auger cable through the overflow.

3 If the drain slows when you reinstall the tripwaste, adjust the tripwaste by shortening the linkage. Tighten the locknut using needle-nose pliers or a wrench.

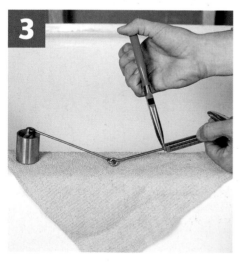

3

SMART TIP

Expect to feel resistance when the cable enters the tub's trap, about 18 inches down. Crank though the blockage, and then retrieve the cable to check for hair.

Clearing a Pop-Up Mechanism

These mechanisms can stretch out of shape over time. So clearing a clog usually means adjusting the linkage as well.

To remove the linkage of a bathtub pop-up drain that's not working properly, grip the plug and pull the linkage out of the drain hole.

Some tripwastes have a plastic adjustment mechanism. Set it to the slot you want, and tighten the locknut using a screwdriver.

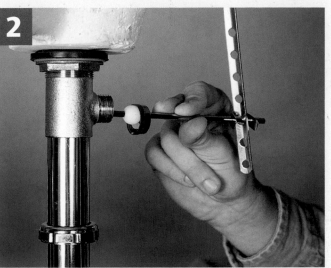

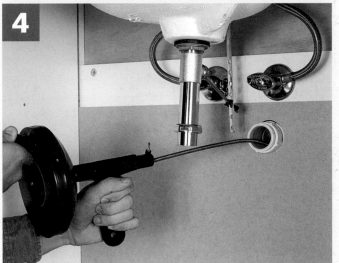

Clearing a Clogged Bathroom Sink Drain

1 When plunging a bathroom sink, cover the overflow hole in the basin with a wet rag.

2 To check for a hair clog on the pop-up plug and lever, loosen the nut, and slide the lever out enough to free the plug.

3 Lift the pop-up plug. You may see a clump of hair clinging to its bottom. Shine a flashlight into the drain, and retrieve a hair clog using wire.

4 If the drain is still clogged, remove a bathroom sink's trap and trap arm, and feed the auger cable directly into the drainage line. Follow with plenty of hot water once you've reassembled the trap.

tools and materials

◆ Plunger ◆ Old Rag ◆ Groove-joint pliers
◆ Auger ◆ Flashlight ◆ Wire

SMART TIP

Pop-up levers have a tendency to clog. To make yours easier to service, install the lever under the pop-up instead of through it. Thereafter, lift out the plug and snag the clog from above.

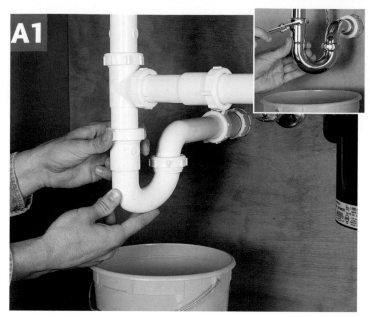

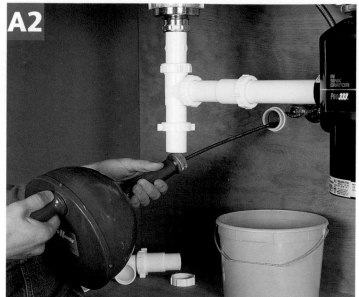

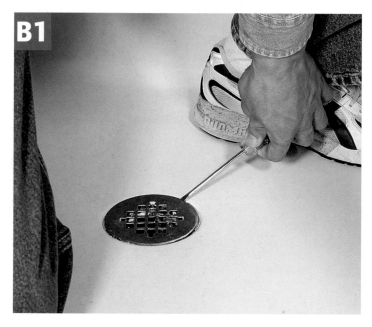

Clearing Other Drains

tools and materials
- Groove-joint pliers
- Pail or bucket
- Drain auger

A1 To gain access to a sink drain, remove the trap and trap arm. Plastic is hand tight, while chrome takes a wrench (inset).

A2 Feed the auger cable into the drain until you feel resistance; then crank through the clog, going forward and back, always cranking clockwise.

B1 For a shower drain, pry up the drain screen with a knife or flat-blade screwdriver if it is not screwed in place.

B2 Insert an auger cable directly into the trap, and turn the handle clockwise as you feed the cable.

C1 To gain access to a floor drain, remove the cleanout plug.

C2 Insert the auger cable directly into the cleanout opening.

Clearing a Toilet

To clear a toilet clog, first use a plunger that has a fold-out cup.

Use a closet auger if you can't clear a clogged toilet using a plunger. Closet augers are designed to work on toilets.

Repelling Tree Roots

Copper sulfate-based drain cleaners are most effective at keeping tree roots out of sewer lines. Copper repels roots, so if you're lucky enough to have large trees in your yard, a once- or twice-a-year treatment is a good idea. It's interesting to note that old-time plumbers sometimes wrapped copper wire around sewer pipe joints.

SMART TIP

When you're clearing a drain, the auger cable may come back coated with black, corrosive goo. To keep the auger working, pull the cable out, hose it down, and spray it with penetrating oil.

Fixing Common Toilet Problems

◆ PROBLEM: SLOW-FILLING TOILET

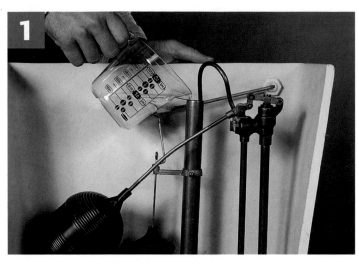

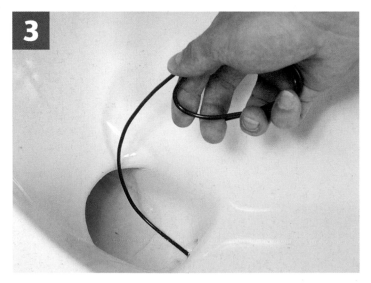

Cleaning a Bacteria-Clogged Toilet

tools and materials

◆ Measuring cup ◆ Bleach solution
◆ Insulated wire ◆ Pocket mirror (if necessary)

Bacteria is a lot like the IRS: It arrives uninvited at the homes of the rich and poor alike, and its hard to get rid of...unless you read the tips below.

1 To kill bacteria buildup in and under the toilet bowl's rim, pour a bleach solution directly into the overflow tube—the open pipe in the tank.

2 Clear bacteria from the rim holes using a short length of electrical wire. Approach the hole from several angles.

3 Clear bacteria from the siphon jet (opposite the trap), using a piece of wire. A dark opening may indicate the presence of bacteria.

Dealing with Mineral Deposits

To remove calcified minerals left by hard water, you'll need slightly different tools. Instead of bleach, pour vinegar into the overflow tube, and let stand for at least 30 minutes.

Vinegar dissolves and loosens mineral deposits, allowing you to break and scrape if from around the rim holes. Vinegar seems to work better when it's heated to about 105 degrees F.

After letting the vinegar stand, ream each hole thoroughly. On heavily clogged holes, use Allen wrenches as reaming tools. Start with a small wrench, and use larger ones as you gradually unclog the hole. Remember that porcelain chips easily, so work carefully and use a pocket mirror to check your work.

f you have never opened the top of a toilet tank until now, you are about to be introduced to the inner workings of your home's most important piece of plumbing, and you are in for a pleasant surprise: many toilet problems are easy to fix. Some problems require a few simple adjustments; others are more complicated to handle. If the inside of your toilet tank does not look like the ones shown here, you probably have a pressure-assisted model. They use water and air pressure to flush away waste, and they are more complicated than the simple gravity-flow toilets shown on these pages.

Removing Grit From the Diaphragm

tools and materials
◆ **Screwdriver**
◆ **Tweezers**

Before taking the steps below, turn off the source water to the tank, and flush the toilet. (The tank shutoff is always near the floor.)

1 This type of fill valve is called a ballcock because it has the traditional float ball attached to it. To reach the diaphragm, remove the brass screws holding it down.

2 With the cover removed, lift the valve's plunger and diaphragm gasket to look for sand, grit, or other sediment.

3 Use tweezers to lift out any sediment particles or rust flakes. You may need to repeat this sequence a time or two over the next month.

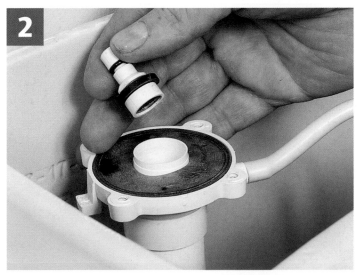

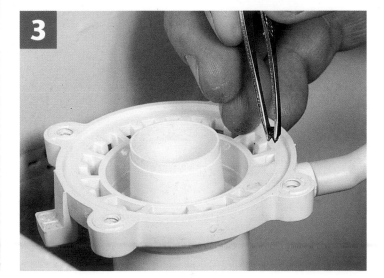

Use a pocket mirror and Allen wrench to ream mineral-clogged holes around the underside of the rim.

PROBLEM: RIPPLING WATER

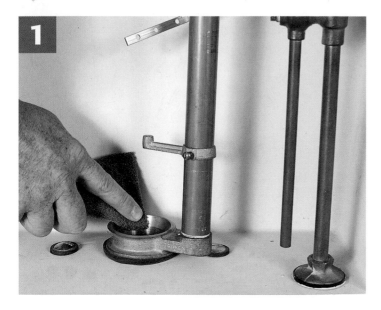

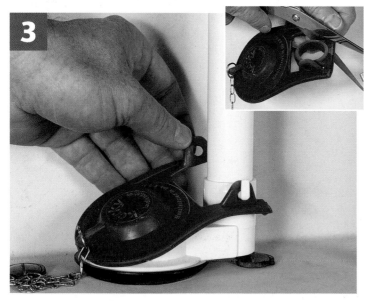

SMART TIP

If you regularly use a chlorine-type toilet tank treatment, expect the tank ball to be somewhat deteriorated and to crumble when you remove it. The chlorine in the treatment tends to degrade rubber.

Replacing a Flapper

tools and materials

◆ Flapper replacement
◆ Abrasive pad, steel wool, or scouring pad
◆ Vinegar (if necessary)
◆ Scissors (if necessary)

A flapper isn't only a dancer from the 1920s, it is also a device that stops the flow of water from the tank into the bowl. If your toilet comes on by itself and then shuts off, or if you hear a steady trickle of water or see ripples in the bowl, you may have a worn flapper or tank ball, opposite.

1 Clean the flush-valve seat by wiping it with an abrasive material such as steel wool or a scouring pad. Feel for imperfections in the seat's surface. You may have to use a little vinegar to dissolve mineral deposits.

2 Universal flush-valve flappers are made to fit either of two situations you'll encounter. If the flush valve has no side pegs at the bottom of the overflow tube, slide the collar over the tube

3 If the overflow tube has side pegs, use scissors to cut off the collar (inset), and hook the eyelets over the pegs. Reconnect the chain.

Replacing a Tank Ball

tools and materials
◆ Slip-joint pliers (if necessary)
◆ Tank ball replacement

At first, a tank ball looks like an antique tool used to predict the weather or barometric pressure. But it is really just a plug that can wear down and needs to be replaced.

1 After you've drained the tank of water, remove the tank ball from the lift wire. The tank ball may crumble if it is more than a few years old.

2 Thread the lift wire into the new tank ball, and check its operation through several flushes. This replacement type has a weighted bottom.

Quick Fixes for Running Toilets

Adjust the flapper chain so that it has about 1 in. of slack.

Adjust the lift-wire support if the tank ball falls off center.

If the overflow tube breaks off, coat the threads of the replacement tube with pipe joint compound before screwing it down.

PROBLEM: A HISSING TOILET

Fixing Valves

The toilet doesn't shut off completely. You hear a hissing noise and see ripples in the bowl. This behavior starts intermittently but over time becomes constant.

Adjust the float rod by bending it downward carefully.

Fine-tune the float by turning its adjustment screw.

On a brass ballcock, replace the rubber seals on the plunger.

SMART TIP

WATER TANK CONDENSATION
If you see water on the floor near the toilet, it may be nothing more than moisture dripping from the sides of the water tank. Condensation on the sides of a tank occurs when air in the room is warm and the humidity is high. The warm air condenses when it meets the cool sides of the tank. Don't take this dripping moisture lightly. If you don't wipe up the puddles (or stop the dripping), water can seep beneath the flooring and cause the subfloor to rot. To prevent condensation problems, buy a toilet-tank insulation kit, which consists of polystyrene (usually) tank liners, from a home center. Shut off the water to the toilet, and drain the tank by flushing. Cut the insulating liners to size; apply the supplied adhesive; and install the liners to the inside of the tank. The polystyrene should prevent the tank sides from becoming so cool that they cause dripping condensation.

PROBLEM: STICKY FLUSH HANDLE

Replacing a Flush Handle

Stiff flush levers are usually heavily corroded, while loose ones are probably broken. You may be able to free a sticking lever using a few drops of penetrating oil, but replacement is a good idea.

There's nothing difficult about this repair, but in this case knowledge works better than leverage: you should know that the hex nut holding a flush lever assembly to the tank uses left-hand threads. (That's right, the threads are backward.) To loosen this nut, turn it clockwise rather than the usual counterclockwise.

Your new lever and handle will likely come in one piece, with the fastening nut the only other component. The lever may be metal or plastic. Snake the lever through the tank hole; then slide the nut over the lever, and screw it onto its threads. Finally, connect the flapper chain or lift wire.

PROBLEM: A STUCK SEAT

Repairing a Stuck Seat

The toilet's seat is broken or worn. You've bought a new seat but can't get the old one off.

This is a common problem when an old toilet seat has brass bolts molded into the seat hinge. When you attempt to loosen the corroded fastening nuts, they stick tight, causing the bolt heads to break loose within their molded sockets. No matter what you do, the bolts just spin. The only way to deal with this situation is to saw through the bolts, just under the seat. To keep from marring the toilet's china surface, place a double thickness of duct tape on the bowl, all around the bolts. Remove the blade from a hacksaw; lay it flat against the bottom of the seat; and cut straight through the bolts.

Tighten the new seat bolt using a screwdriver, and snap the hinged cover in place.

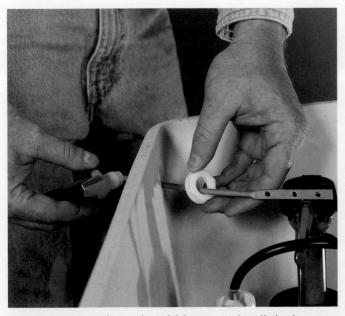

Remove the nut from the old lever, and pull the lever through the tank hole.

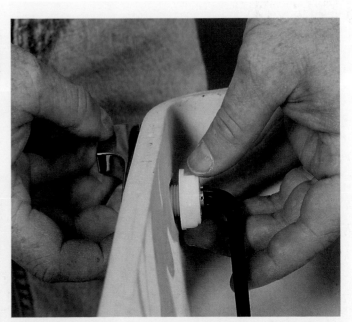

Slide the new lever in place, and tighten the nut. The nut has left-hand threads.

Working with Plastic Pipe

I f you can learn to keep the primer and glue off your hands (try surgical gloves), working with plastic pipe is easy to master. It cuts like butter, sands down like wood with hardly any effort, and can be glued together like a child's toy. Because the plastic couplings dictate the pipe angles with precision, even your first attempt could look like the work of a professional. Promise. Unlike copper, which can take some tricky soldering and requires the use of torches in close spaces, plastic is very forgiving. Plus, even if you screw up the entire project, it doesn't cost much to trash the work entirely, recycle the pipes, and start over. Also, supply lines and drainpipes are all made of similar plastic material, and they are assembled with the same primer and glue. One tip: never glue anything until you have cut and assembled the pipe configuration in a dry run.

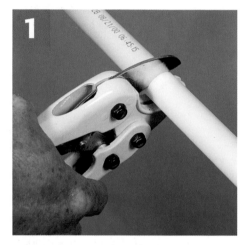

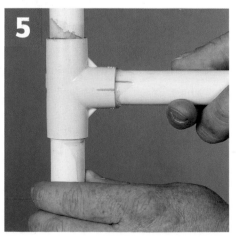

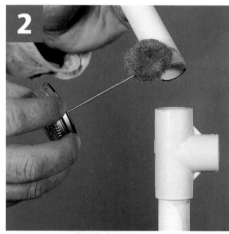

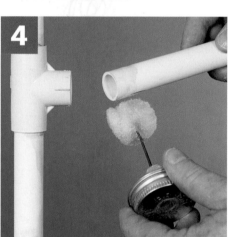

Cutting and Fitting CPVP Pipe

tools and materials

- ◆ **Pipe-cutting shears**
- ◆ **CPVC pipe & fittings**
- ◆ **CPVC solvent primer**
- ◆ **CPVC solvent cement**
- ◆ **Pencil** ◆ **Measuring tape**

1 Use plastic-pipe-cutting shears to cut CPVC. Be sure to allow for the depth of the fitting hub. This tool makes the cleanest possible cut.

2 Apply primer to the pipe ends and fitting hubs. Primer removes the surface glaze and reduces leaks. Use sandpaper if you don't have primer.

3 Test-fit the pipe and fittings. Before you disassemble the pipe and cement it, mark the final alignment using a pencil.

4 Apply CPVC solvent cement to the pipe and fitting hub, and insert the pipe about one-quarter turn out of alignment.

5 Rotate the pipe one-quarter turn after inserting it to line up the pencil marks. This spreads the cement and accelerates curing.

SMART TIP

Most plumbing codes accept plastic pipe for use in drain lines, but not all accept it for supply lines. Before changing your piping, call your local building department for clarification.

Plastic Drainage Piping

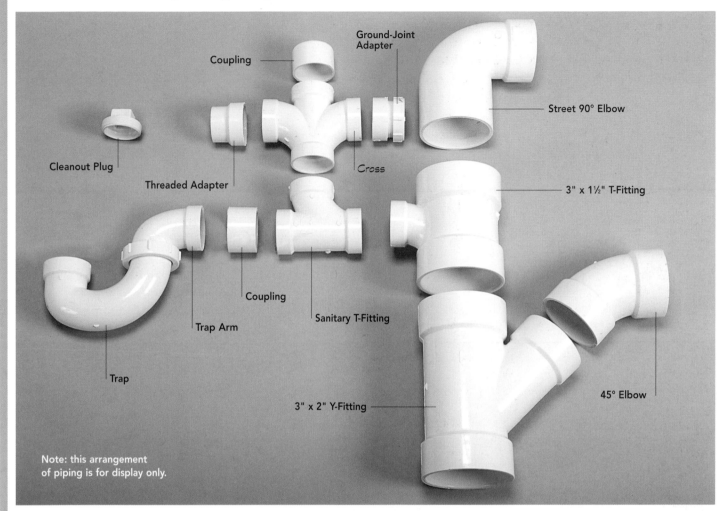

Coupling

Ground-Joint Adapter

Street 90° Elbow

Cleanout Plug

Cross

Threaded Adapter

3" x 1½" T-Fitting

Coupling

Sanitary T-Fitting

Trap Arm

Trap

45° Elbow

3" x 2" Y-Fitting

Note: this arrangement
of piping is for display only.

Getting
Clean Cuts

1 Cut the pipe using a hacksaw
(as shown at right), or you
can also use a handsaw, special PVC saw, wheel cutter, or
power miter saw. Be sure the
cut is straight.

2 Use an inexpensive deburring
tool or the rounded side of a
file to smooth the ragged
edge left by the saw. This is
a necessary step or the pipe
won't fit the fitting correctly.

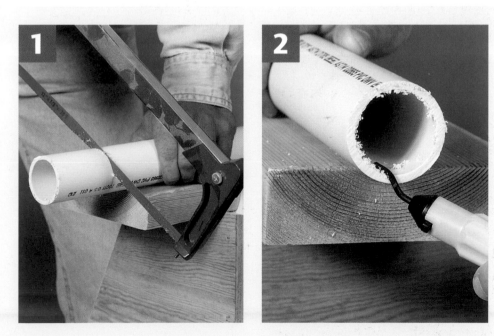

Working with Copper Pipe

Be warned: this is plumbing for grown-ups. Copper is a highly versatile and stable plumbing material, but it takes practice and specialty tools to do it right. If you are uncomfortable with fire in close spaces, red-hot torches, molten solder, cutting metal, or working with hot pipes, you show a healthy respect for the medium. But don't let it stop you. The instructions shown here can help you get over your fears. Plus, if you learn copper work, or "sweating joints," your circle of friends with plumbing problems will expand exponentially.

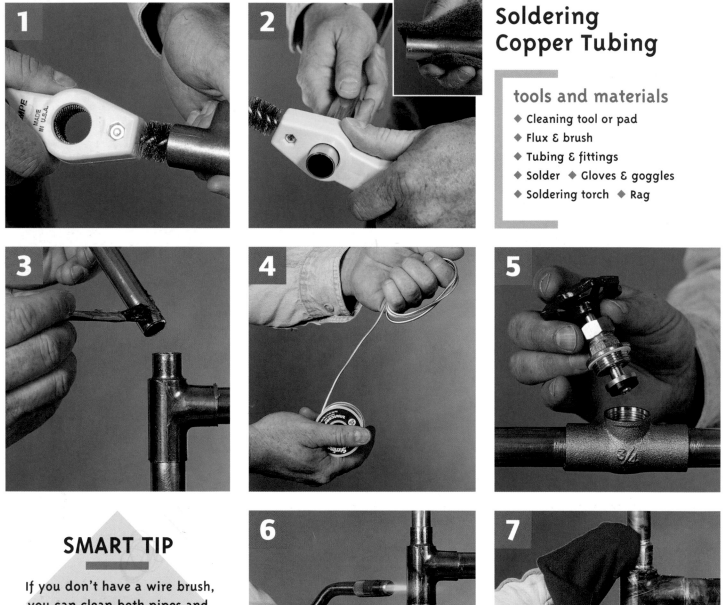

Soldering Copper Tubing

tools and materials

- ◆ Cleaning tool or pad
- ◆ Flux & brush
- ◆ Tubing & fittings
- ◆ Solder ◆ Gloves & goggles
- ◆ Soldering torch ◆ Rag

SMART TIP

If you don't have a wire brush, you can clean both pipes and fittings with a soap-free household abrasive scrubbing pad. Force the pad into the fitting hubs with your finger.

SMART TIP

The trick to using a tubing cutter is not to start the wheel too deep. Just tighten it until it feels snug, and retighten when it feels loose.

1 Use a combination tool, wire brush, or abrasive pad to clean each hub on the fitting. Combination tools have two different brush sizes.

2 Scour the end of each pipe shiny, working at least 1 in. back from where the fitting will be attached. Wipe the pipe and fitting with a rag.

3 Apply flux to the pipe end and the inside of the fitting using a small brush. Insert the pipe, and wipe away the excess flux.

4 Pull approximately 24 in. of solder from the spool, and wrap it around your hand for a more comfortable grip.

5 To keep from scorching the rubber and plastic parts in a shutoff valve, remove the stem before soldering the valve.

6 Heat both sides of the lowest hub on the fitting. Touch the solder to the fitting. Continue to heat the fitting until the solder starts to melt.

7 When you've finished soldering the fitting and before the solder hardens, wipe the excess solder from each joint. Wipe away from yourself. Test your work after the pipe cools.

Cutting Copper

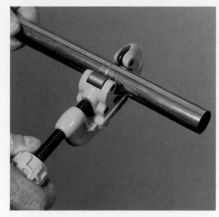

Tighten the wheel cutter to clamp it onto the pipe. Rotate the cutter with the wheel following the rollers.

You can use a miniature hacksaw as you would a full-size one because it fits into tight spaces.

No-Solder Connections

Compression-type water fittings are usually used to connect a supply line to a shutoff valve among other uses. They consist of a brass body—either an adapter body or valve body—with two or more pipe hubs. The fitting hubs have external threads and beveled rims. The nuts are open at the top so that you can insert pipes through them. A third component, a brass compression ring called a ferrule, makes the seal. The ferrule is also beveled, top and bottom. (The external threads, the nut, and the brass ferrule are visible in the top photo.)

Make the connection by sliding the nut and ferrule onto the end of a pipe; insert the pipe into the fitting hub; and tighten. The beveled surfaces force the ring inward, cinching it around the pipe. The ring crushes the pipe a little; it locks the ring in place and makes the water seal.

Coat the ferrule and threads using pipe joint compound.

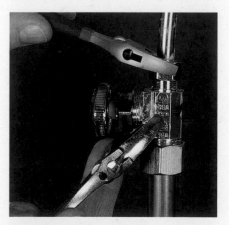

Hold the valve using one wrench, and tighten with the other.

Dealing with Plumbing Emergencies

Stuff, as they say, happens. And if often happens to plumbing systems. The most common plumbing emergency is a burst pipe. Sometimes this is a small pinhole leak in an old cast-iron pipe, and sometimes it is a full-blown gusher coming from a gash in a copper pipe. You can stop some leaks by tightening a fitting; other repairs require a patch of some sort. The solution to most plumbing emergencies start the same way: turn off the water. Then you can assess the problem and make the repair, or call a plumber knowing you've limited the damage.

Frozen Pipes

Apply heat using a hair dryer when dealing with frozen pipes. Be sure to insulate all pipes that run through unheated areas.

Frozen pipes are scary. Water expands as it freezes, and it could cause the pipe to burst. Even if it didn't expand, a block of ice stops water from flowing through the pipes to get to faucets and other fixtures.

In your desperation to thaw a frozen pipe, it's tempting to grab the tool that will quickly deliver maximum heat, such as an open-flamed torch. Bad idea. Torching the pipes will melt the ice within, but it can also boil the water. The pressure created can split the pipe seam, or — through the expansion and contraction that accompanies heating and cooling — weaken the pipe so that it bursts later, such as when you're at work or on vacation.

To thaw a pipe, open the nearest faucet, and apply heat using a hair dryer, non-open-flame space heater, or by wrapping the pipes in hot towels that you change regularly. Check all other faucets in your home to find out if you have additional frozen pipes. If one pipe has frozen, others may have frozen, too.

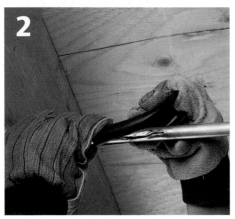

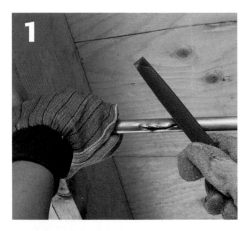

Temporary Repairs

tools and materials
◆ Metal file
◆ Screwdriver
◆ Rubber pipe insulation
◆ Banded clamps

A temporary patch like the one shown left should be tested under full pressure and watched closely, especially when pressure surges through the typical on-off cycles of such items as garden hoses, showers, and dishwashers

1 To make a temporary repair that won't leak, first use a file to flatten out any ragged edges around the split.

2 Slit a thick piece of rubber or a short section of garden hose, and slip it over the damaged pipe.

3 Attach banded clamps over the rubber sleeve at each end of the split, and tighten the clamp screws.

You might think it strange to see a section on water heaters in a book dedicated to simple repairs and improvements. That would be true if we were discussing replacing a water heater or running a new gas line for a gas-powered unit. But as with any complicated piece of equipment, there are a variety of simple things that can solve minor inconveniences and ward off potential major problems. That is what we discuss here. For other problems, call in a plumber.

SMART TIP

One way to help your water heater last longer is to periodically drain any sediment that builds up inside it. To drain the water heater, turn the gas control to "Pilot;" turn off the electrical power; and shut off the water to the unit. Connect a hose to the drain valve, and place the other end near a floor drain. Open the drain valve. After a few minutes, turn the water back on while still draining. Repeat a few times. Finally, close the drain and fill the tank half full; then drain again. Note: scale is produced faster in temperatures above 130 degrees.

WATER-HEATER PROBLEMS

Replacing a Sediment-Clogged Drain Valve

If you find that the drain fitting drips, especially after clearing out the water heater, sediment is probably blocking the stop mechanism. You may be able to get rid of the sediment by operating the valve under pressure. If not, replace the drain valve. Start by turning the gas control to "Pilot" or turning off the electricity at the electrical panel and letting the water cool until it's comfortable. (There's no need to drain the tank if all of the faucets remain closed.) If the drain valve is a standard hose bibcock, just back it from the tank using a wrench.

Remove the leaky old drain valve using large groove-joint pliers.

Install a new valve, turning it clockwise. Use pipe-thread sealing tape or pipe joint compound on the threads.

Keep a Lid on Tank Pressure

The T&P valve keeps pressure from building up in the water heater. Test it every six months. Just lift the test lever, and let it snap back. There should be a momentary blast of hot water through the valve's overflow tube. No water? Valve stuck? Replace the valve. Shut off the water, and let it cool for a few hours. Open a faucet and the tank's drain until the water is below the T&P valve. Follow the steps below to remove and replace the value. When complete, attach a length of pipe that runs from the valve to a floor drain.

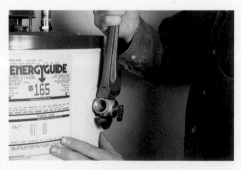
Test the T&P valve periodically. Remove it if it seizes up or doesn't seem to work properly.

Wrap the threads using pipe-thread sealing tape, and tighten the valve into the opening.

6
Electrical Projects

Charting Electrical Circuits

Identifying which circuits service all the receptacles, switches, lights, and appliances in your house takes some time. Working with a helper is best, so you'll have to draft someone for the afternoon and expel everyone else so things are quiet. The helper will come in handy when you check for circuits that supply such things as ceiling fans and appliances. The time and effort you spend on this job, however, are well worth it. By knowing which breaker controls which device, you can quickly turn off power to anything you are working on and avoid the risk of serious shock. It is actually much easier if you communicate with your helper through walkie-talkies or even cell phones. It's important that you identify each circuit with the corresponding outlet that it controls.

SMART TIP

Small, inexpensive circuit testers or "multi-testers" really come in handy when determining if outlets are "hot" (energized). The testers have two leads that are inserted into the outlet to spot check for power.

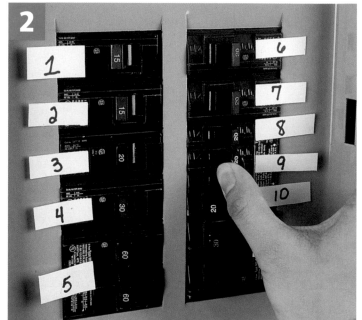

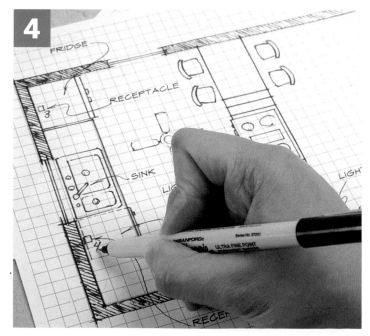

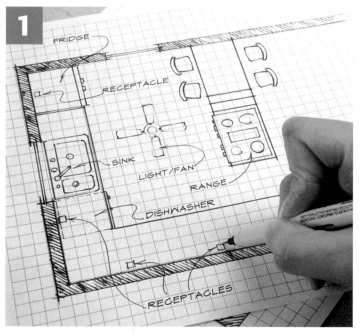

Creating a Circuit Map

tools and materials
◆ Felt tip marker
◆ Stick-on labels
◆ Graph paper
◆ Ruler
◆ Circuit list for panel door

1 Before you label anything in your service panel box, make a scaled drawing of every room in your house. Draw the location of all the receptacles, light fixtures, switches, and appliances.

2 Once all the circuits are identified, go to the service panel and mark which breakers go to which circuits using stick-on labels. Then test each circuit by turning off the power, plugging in a radio (that's turned on) to any given outlet, and then turning the power on at the panel to see if the radio plays.

3 If you are working by yourself, adjust the radio to a high volume so that you can hear it from the panel.

4 As you go from outlet to outlet, note on your room drawings which ones occupy which circuits.

5 You will also need help from someone to check any appliance circuits, such as an electric range.

Breaker Types

A single-pole breaker is the most prevalent type in residential use. It will power anything that requires 120-volt current.

A double-pole breaker is used with a 240-volt appliance, such as a 20-amp baseboard heater or a 30-amp clothes dryer.

Use a quad breaker to serve two double-pole circuits in the same space as one standard double-pole breaker.

A GFCI circuit breaker will cut power to a circuit when it is tripped by an imbalance in current flow through the wires.

A surge-protection device provides protection for an entire service panel and simply installs in place of two single-pole breakers.

Working with Wires and Cable

The most common form of cable in U.S. households is nonmetallic cable, often referred to by its brand name, Romex. In a typical house, the cable contains two or three individual wires and a bare copper wire. The white plastic jacket is aligned so that it can be slit open with a razor without damaging the wires strands within. The white jacket of the cable is also printed with information. It states the gauge of the wires inside the jacket—the lower the number the more power it can handle. A typical light circuit usually uses 14-gauge wire; a more powerful appliance circuit uses 12-gauge wire. The color-sheathed wires carry the power and complete the electric circuit; the bare wire is the ground. If there is a short circuit in the system, the bare wire conducts the electrical power back to the breaker box. The box is connected to a cold-water pipe and a grounding electrode.

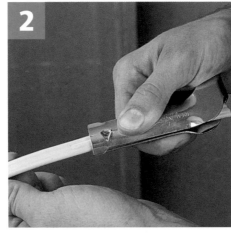

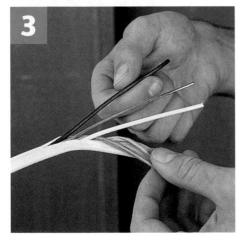

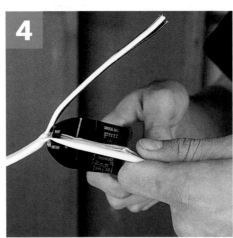

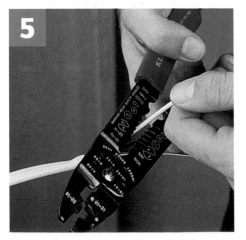

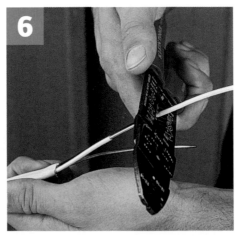

Stripping Cable Sheathing

tools and materials

- ◆ Cable ripper
- ◆ Combination tool
- ◆ Cable

1 Slide the cable ripper onto the cable, and squeeze it 8 to 10 in. from the end to force the point through the plastic sheath.

2 Grip the cable tool in one hand and the cable in the other, and pull the ripper toward the end of the cable.

3 Expose wires by peeling back the plastic sheathing and paper wrapping. A cable ripper won't damage individual wires.

4 Use a combination tool's cutting jaws to trim away excess plastic sheathing and paper wrapping inside the sheath.

5 Use the cutting jaws of the combination tool to cut individual wires in the cable to length, if needed.

6 A combination tool has slots for different gauges of wire. The correct one will remove the sheath without crimping the wire.

Attaching Wires

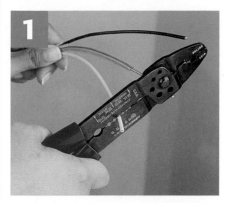

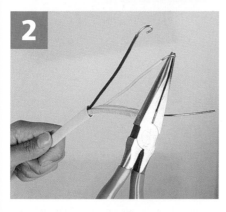

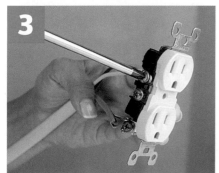

1 Clamp the wire in the proper gauge slot of a combination tool, and strip ¾ in. of insulation from each wire end.

2 Use needle-nose pliers to form a clockwise half-loop at the end of each wire. Avoid making nicks that could weaken the wire.

3 Hook the looped wire end onto the screw terminal. The clockwise wire loop will close as you tighten the screw.

SMART TIP

Most home wiring systems use copper wire, but aluminum has been used in the past. If your house has copper-clad wires, do not add aluminum wires to it, use copper instead. Also, use only receptacles, such as outlets and switches, marked CO/ALR with aluminum wiring systems.

Types of Wires

Wires and cables have different weights, thicknesses, and jackets for specific reasons. A bare wire is invariably used as a ground and nothing else. Armored cable is suited for areas that will experience wear, exposure, or heat.

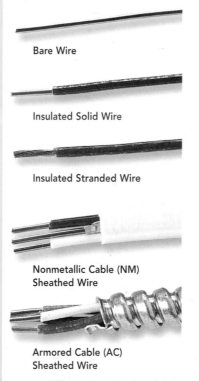

Bare Wire

Insulated Solid Wire

Insulated Stranded Wire

Nonmetallic Cable (NM) Sheathed Wire

Armored Cable (AC) Sheathed Wire

Capping Wires

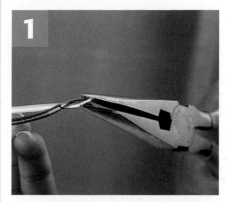

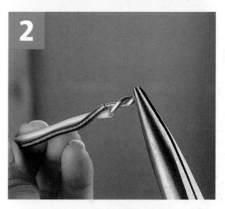

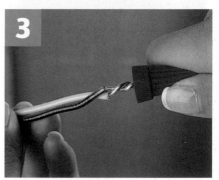

1 To join wires, strip ½ in. of insulation; hold the wires parallel; and twist them together clockwise using pliers.

2 The twisted part should be long enough to engage the wire connector without exposing any bare wire when it is applied.

3 Screw down on a wire connector so that the exposed wires are covered. Use hand pressure only, not the force of pliers.

Replacing an Outlet Receptacle

R eplace, or have replaced, any outlet receptacle that is damaged or not working properly. Problem receptacles are dangerous. We show how to wire an end-of-run receptacle below. That means it is the last outlet in a series and there is only one cable entering the box. A middle-of-run receptacle looks like the one shown opposite. To replace an existing receptacle, purchase one with the same rating as the original. Always turn off the power and test the outlet to make sure it is not "hot" (use a circuit tester) before you even remove the plate that grants you access to the receptacle box. When removing the receptacle, inspect the wires to make sure the jackets are not cracked.

SMART TIP

If adding new cable to a box, allow yourself a healthy 6 to 8 inches of cable with which to work. The processes of stripping wires of their insulation and making connections shorten the cable, so start with a reasonable amount.

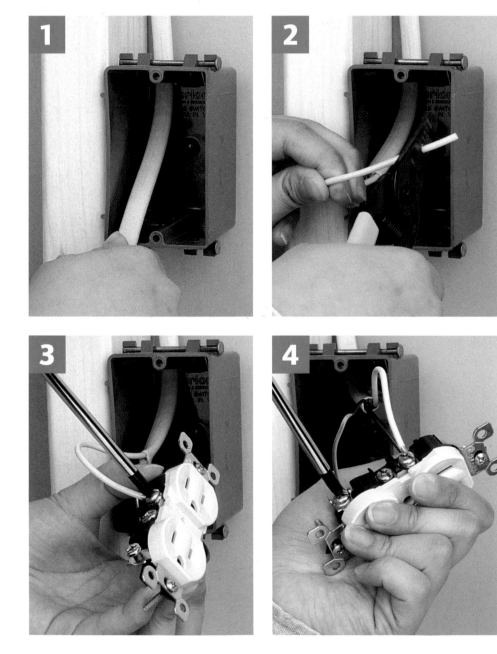

Wiring an End-of-Run Receptacle

tools and materials
- Flat-head screwdriver
- Needle-nose pliers
- Lineman's pliers
- Wire strippers
- Circuit tester

1 Pull approximately 6 in. of wire cable into the receptacle box. Plastic boxes like this have a built-in clip to hold the cable in place.

2 Strip the cable sheathing no closer than ½ in. from the clamp inside the receptacle box.

3 Loop the stripped wires clockwise two-thirds of the way around their respective screw terminals; then tighten the screws. (See "Receptacle Connections," opposite.)

4 Fold the wires and center the receptacle in the box. Screw it to the box through the center holes. Add the cover plate.

Other Receptacles

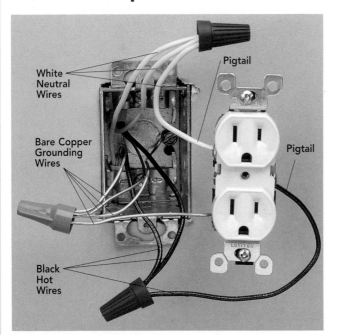

White Neutral Wires

Pigtail

Bare Copper Grounding Wires

Pigtail

Black Hot Wires

This type of connection, using a metal box, allows the receptacles on a circuit to be wired independently.

Receptacles may be wired in these three ways: (See Receptacle Types, top right.)

Non-grounded, non-polarized receptacles have two identical slots, side by side. One slot is not bigger than the other, as with modern outlets, and therefore the slots are not polarized. In this case, it is impossible to tell which one is hot and which one is neutral. These kinds of older receptacles should be replaced at the first opportunity.

Non-grounded polarized receptacles have two slots, one larger than the other, but no slot for a ground plug. Electrical devices that can be used with non-grounded receptacles include lamps, radios, power adapters, vacuum cleaners, and items have no third round prong on their plugs. Electrical devices that require a grounded receptacle are appliances, computers, TV's, stereo equipment, power tools, surge protector strips, and any electrical devices with a third prong.

Grounded receptacles are the safest receptacles, because they accommodate a ground wire combined with slots that are not the same size, so the receptacle can be polarized. These are the receptacles that the National Electrical Codes require for installation in most situations.

Receptacle Types

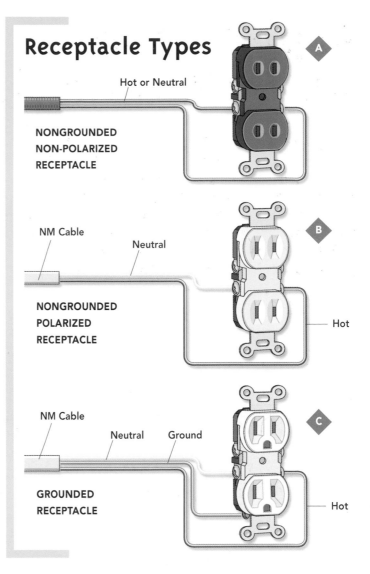

Hot or Neutral

NONGROUNDED NON-POLARIZED RECEPTACLE

A

NM Cable

Neutral

NONGROUNDED POLARIZED RECEPTACLE

Hot

B

NM Cable

Neutral   Ground

GROUNDED RECEPTACLE

Hot

C

Receptacle Connections

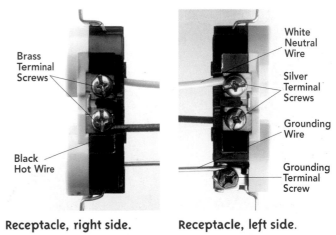

Brass Terminal Screws

Black Hot Wire

White Neutral Wire

Silver Terminal Screws

Grounding Wire

Grounding Terminal Screw

Receptacle, right side. Connect hot black or red wires to the brass terminal screws.

Receptacle, left side. Connect white wires to the silver terminals; the green screw receives the ground.

GFCI Receptacles

A ground-fault circuit interrupter (GFCI) is a safety device that shuts down the power in a circuit in 1/25th of a second. In a normal circuit, power flows to a device through the black wire and returns through the white neutral wire. As long as the power is balanced between the two, everything is fine. If there is a mishap, say a loose connection, and the power is not balanced between the hot and neutral wires, the GFCI senses the imbalance and stops the power. GFCI protection is required by the National Electrical Code in wet locations, such as near sinks, laundry rooms, and outdoors.

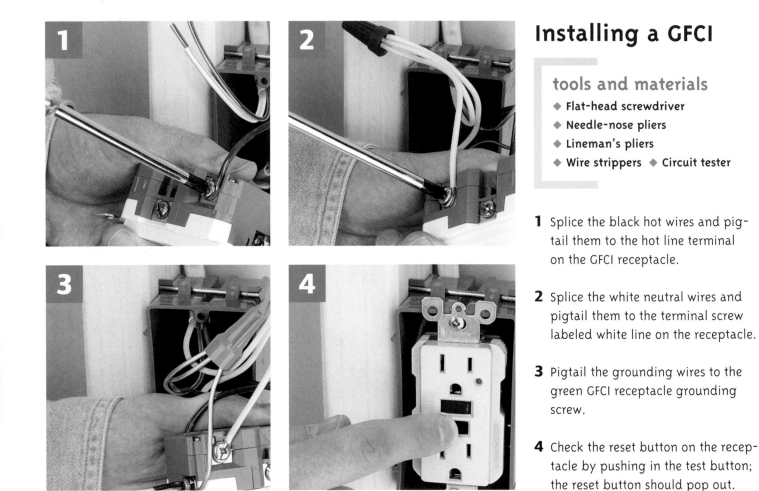

Installing a GFCI

tools and materials
- ◆ Flat-head screwdriver
- ◆ Needle-nose pliers
- ◆ Lineman's pliers
- ◆ Wire strippers ◆ Circuit tester

1 Splice the black hot wires and pigtail them to the hot line terminal on the GFCI receptacle.

2 Splice the white neutral wires and pigtail them to the terminal screw labeled white line on the receptacle.

3 Pigtail the grounding wires to the green GFCI receptacle grounding screw.

4 Check the reset button on the receptacle by pushing in the test button; the reset button should pop out.

Testing Devices

Use a continuity tester on wiring and appliances to pinpoint trouble by determining if a complete circuit exists.

Some analyzers can test for power, reversed wire connections, and other conditions of your electrical system.

GFCI Protection

A **GFCI receptacle** has both test and reset buttons. When a ground fault occurs or a test is made, the reset button will pop out. Once a fault is eliminated or the test completed, press the button back in to reset the circuit.

A **GFCI circuit breaker** has a test button, but no reset button. To reset a GFCI breaker, first push the switch to the off position; then flip it back to the on position. These breakers protect the entire circuit.

Using GFCI Outlets Outdoors

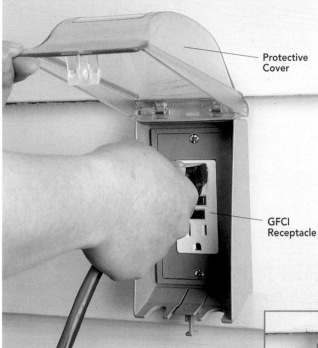

Protective Cover

GFCI Receptacle

Outdoor equipment in constant and unattended use must be connected to a weatherproof box. The cover must protect the box even when the plug is in use.

SMART TIP

Working outdoors? Plug your tools into a GFCI extension cord. These special cords offer the same safety protection that a GFCI outlet offers.

Multi-Location Protection

A **GFCI receptacle** for multilocation protection will have one set of hot and neutral wires connected to the line terminal screws and the other to the load terminal screws.

Replacing a Light Switch

A faulty switch can cause electric shock or a fire. As with any electrical work, always turn off the circuit that energizes the switch. Remove the switch, and check the copper wire for any metal fatigue that might have occurred when the wire was bent to fit around the screw terminals. Check the wire insulation to make sure it is intact. If the switch is in the middle of a series, only the black wires are connected to the switch; if at the end of the line, shown opposite, connect both the black and white wires, but tape the white wire to show it is hot. If the switch still does not work, call an electrician.

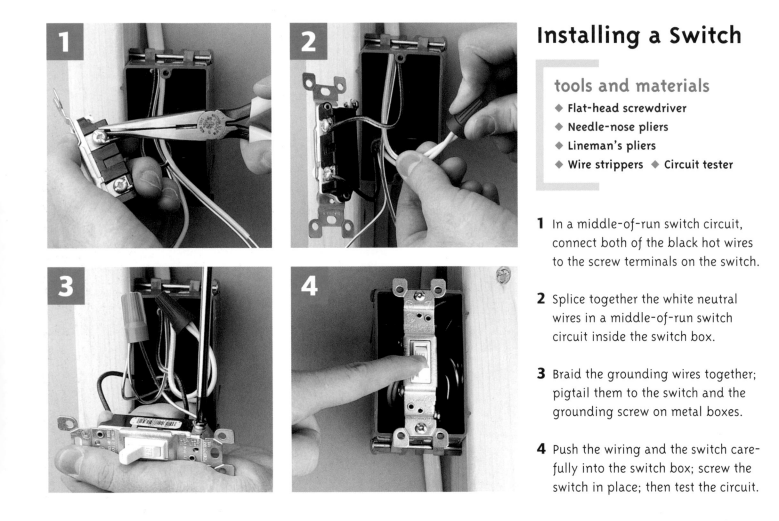

Installing a Switch

> ### tools and materials
> ◆ Flat-head screwdriver
> ◆ Needle-nose pliers
> ◆ Lineman's pliers
> ◆ Wire strippers ◆ Circuit tester

1 In a middle-of-run switch circuit, connect both of the black hot wires to the screw terminals on the switch.

2 Splice together the white neutral wires in a middle-of-run switch circuit inside the switch box.

3 Braid the grounding wires together; pigtail them to the switch and the grounding screw on metal boxes.

4 Push the wiring and the switch carefully into the switch box; screw the switch in place; then test the circuit.

Testing a Switch

When you flip on a switch and the switch circuit doesn't work, the problem may not be with the switch. It could be a blown fuse, a tripped circuit breaker, or a faulty fixture. First check the service panel; then test the switch. Remove the fuse or turn off the breaker; then remove the switch coverplate. Use a circuit tester to verify that the power is turned off; then turn on the switch. Next, touch the probe and clip of a battery-operated continuity tester to the wire terminals. If the switch is good, the tester will light up or buzz. Turn off the switch. If it is good, then the tester should no longer light up or buzz. Replace the switch if it fails any of these tests. If the switch is good, the fault must be in the fixture.

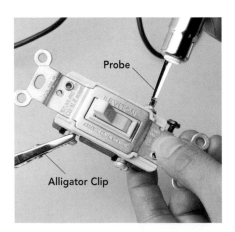

Probe

Alligator Clip

Types of Switches

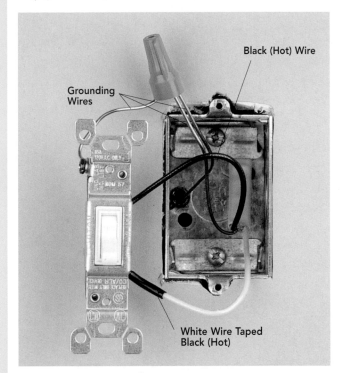

At the end of a circuit, both the black and white wires connecting to a switch are hot. To indicate this, wrap the white wire with black tape.

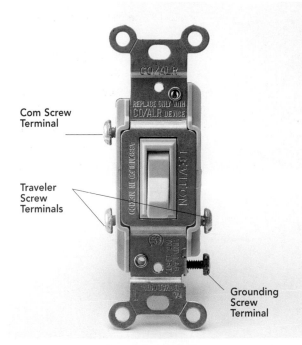

Three-way switches are used when two switches control the same fixture or light. These switches have three terminal screws and no on/off positions. Wires attached to the traveler terminals connect the two switches together.

Single-Pole Switch to Light Fixture

In a standard lighting circuit, the power is supplied by a two-wire cable with a grounding wire. In this configuration, the light fixture is located at the end of the cable run.

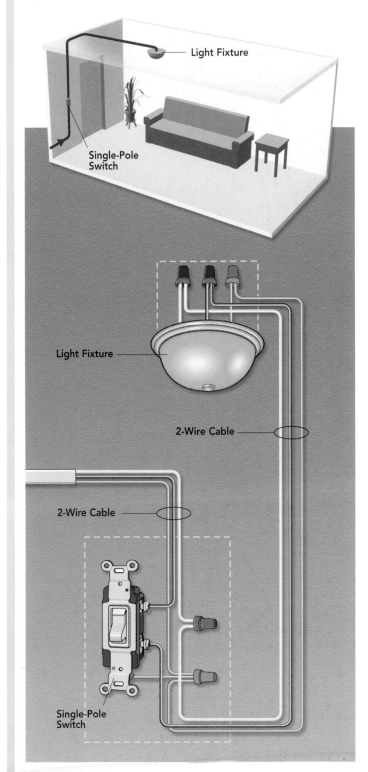

Low-Voltage Outdoor Lighting

Low-voltage lighting uses household power that has been "stepped down" by a transformer from 120 volts to the desired low voltage, usually about 12 volts. This makes the wires extremely safe, but it still pays to be careful when making electrical connections. You can purchase lighting kits that include the transformer, wires, and fixtures. Or you can buy the components separately, creating a custom lighting scheme. Products vary, but in most cases you run the wiring from the transformer to the fixtures, make the connections, and bury the cable in a few inches of soil.

Installing Low-Voltage Lighting

tools and materials

- Flat-head screwdriver
- Needle-nose pliers
- Lineman's pliers
- Wire strippers
- Circuit tester

1 Make a cutout in an exterior wall for a retrofit switch/GFCI receptacle box.

2 Attach hot and neutral wires in the GFCI receptacle box. Pigtail the ground wires to the grounding screw.

3 Position your low-voltage lighting system along a walk, drive, or other landscaping feature.

4 Lay the cable in a trench at least 6 in. deep, and clip the wire fixture leads to the cable.

5 Following the manufacturer's directions, connect the low-voltage wires to the 12-volt step-down transformer.

6 Plug the transformer into the GFCI receptacle; turn on the power; and test the lights.

Low-Voltage Fixture Options

GARDEN LIGHTS

SOLAR LIGHT

SAFETY LIGHTS

STEP LIGHTS

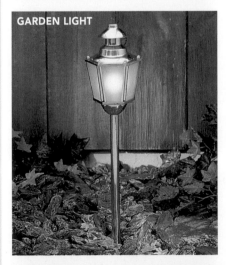

GARDEN LIGHT

MUSHROOM LIGHT

PATH LIGHTING

UPLIGHTING

Surface Wiring

Installing Surface Wiring

The hardest part about any electrical project in an existing house involves fishing wires through finished walls. It is difficult, and you usually need to make major repairs to the walls. That's where a surface wiring system comes in. You encase the cable in a metal channel that you attach to the surface of the wall. This is your only option for masonry walls.

tools and materials

- ◆ **Flat-head & Phillips head screwdrivers**
- ◆ **Needle-nose pliers** ◆ **Lineman's pliers**
- ◆ **Wire strippers** ◆ **Circuit tester** ◆ **Snips**

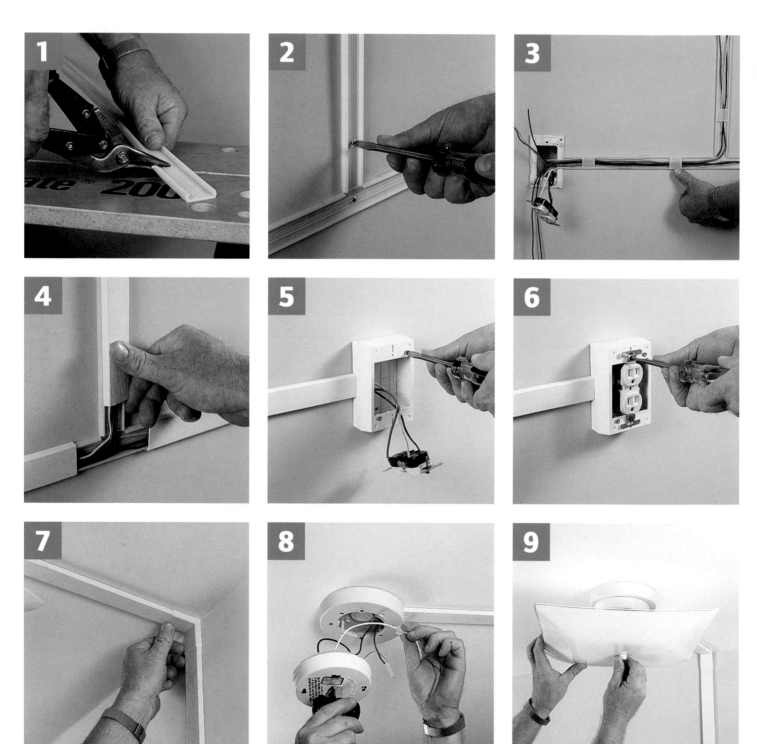

1 Plastic surface wire channels, called raceways, are easy to cut—use metal snips on the base channel and a hacksaw on trim.

2 Screw the base channel to the wall with plastic anchors. At a tee, clip the edge to clear a path for wires.

3 Install a box plate over an existing outlet, and extend wires from that circuit. Hold the wires using clips.

4 Once all wiring is in place, clip trim channel over the tracks. There are special connectors for T- and L-joints.

5 Where raceway wiring feeds power to a new outlet, you can mount a matching plastic outlet box on the wall.

6 Strip the wire leads; connect them to the terminals on the outlet; and screw the outlet to the plastic wall box.

7 To feed power to a ceiling light, run a raceway up the wall and across to the fixture. Cover the corner using an L-clip.

8 Raceway systems have surface mounts for outlets and switches—and ceiling fixtures. Connect the leads using wire connectors.

9 Once the wiring is complete, screw the fixture base to the raceway ceiling mount, and fasten the diffuser to the fixture.

Running Cables in Walls

One way to run cable across a wall is to make several cutouts in the drywall to expose the wall studs; then bore holes through the center of the studs using an angled drill. Fish the cable from the existing box to the new location. When finished, patch the cutouts. Be sure you know what is inside a wall before cutting into it. Avoid working around ducts, plumbing, and other wiring.

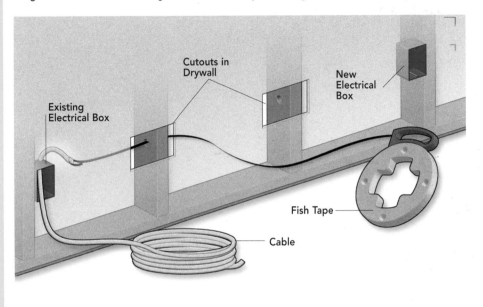

Cutouts in Drywall

New Electrical Box

Existing Electrical Box

Fish Tape

Cable

SMART TIP

FISHING CONNECTIONS
Fish tape is a lifesaver when you do need to run cable through walls and between floors. This flexible material comes in 50- and 100-foot rolls. When threading wire using fish tape, it is tempting to cut a large hole, but cut the hole as small as possible to save on the repair time.

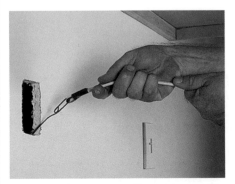

Instead of trying to thread bendable cable through wall cavities, thread a more controllable steel fish tape.

Bend wire leads around the fish tape hook; tape the leads down; and roll up the tape to pull the cable through.

Repairing Plugs

Because plugs are often molded into the extension cord wires, it is tempting to throw out an extension cord with a faulty plug. But the extension cord can be saved by adding a replacement plug. Plugs match the use for which they are intended. Generally, large, round plugs that have a grounding prong are used for large appliances. The grounding prong is an integral part of the assembly. Without it, a short circuit in an appliance or a tool that you may be using would become a dangerous hazard. To add a new plug, cut the cord behind the plug, and follow the directions below.

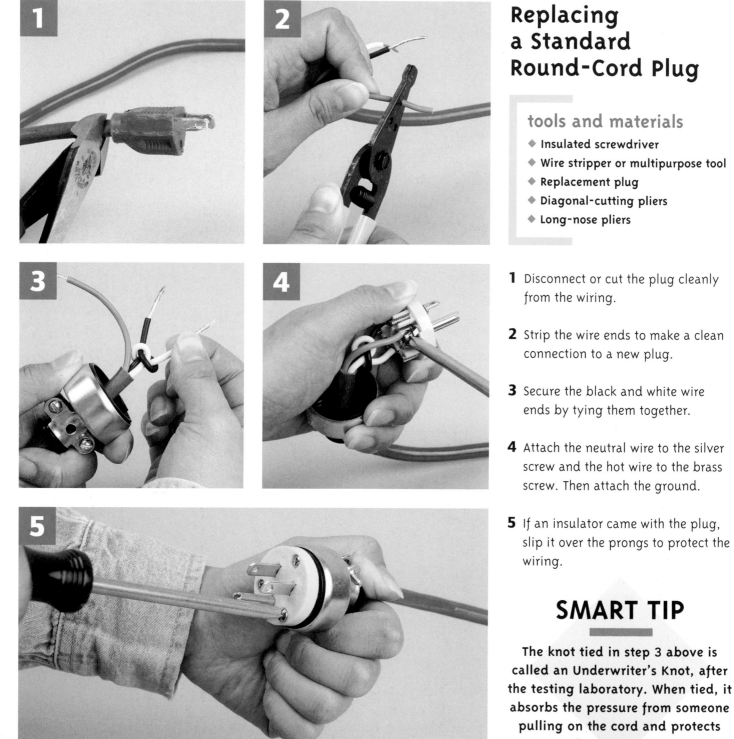

Replacing a Standard Round-Cord Plug

tools and materials

- ◆ Insulated screwdriver
- ◆ Wire stripper or multipurpose tool
- ◆ Replacement plug
- ◆ Diagonal-cutting pliers
- ◆ Long-nose pliers

1 Disconnect or cut the plug cleanly from the wiring.

2 Strip the wire ends to make a clean connection to a new plug.

3 Secure the black and white wire ends by tying them together.

4 Attach the neutral wire to the silver screw and the hot wire to the brass screw. Then attach the ground.

5 If an insulator came with the plug, slip it over the prongs to protect the wiring.

SMART TIP

The knot tied in step 3 above is called an Underwriter's Knot, after the testing laboratory. When tied, it absorbs the pressure from someone pulling on the cord and protects the connection.

Installing a Quick-Connect Plug

1 On flat cord, simply disconnect or cut away the old plug. Cut an inch or two behind the plug.

2 Insert unstripped wires into the prongs of a quick-connect plug.

3 Squeeze the plug prongs together, and secure the cover. Prongs on the inside of the plug core piece will pierce the wires to make the connection. Snap the plug core into its casing.

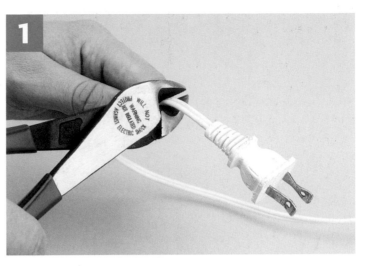

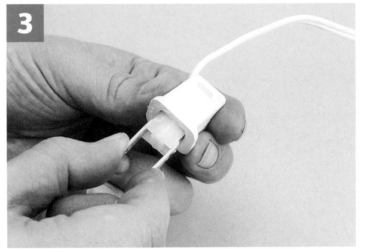

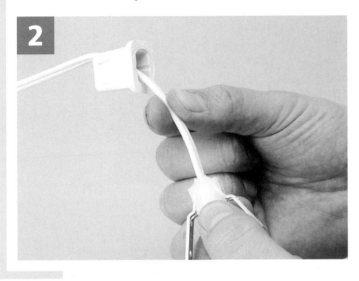

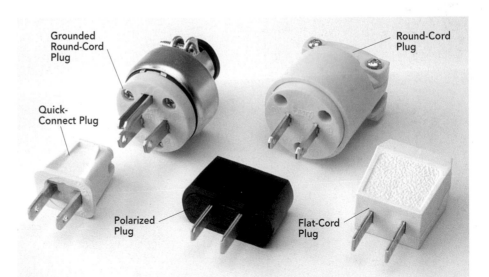

Plugs, Cords, and Sockets

The reason that plugs come in a wide variety of styles is not just to make your house look more interesting. Each type of plug is designed in a specific way to accomplish a specific task. Heavy duty three-prong plugs are for tools or appliances that draw lots of amperage. They also can endure wear and tear in demanding settings. Lightweight plugs that you see on lamp cords tend to be smaller because of the power they deliver and the way they are used.

Grounded Round-Cord Plug

Round-Cord Plug

Quick-Connect Plug

Polarized Plug

Flat-Cord Plug

Plugs come in various configurations for different purposes; be sure that the replacement plugs that you buy are appropriate for the appliances, receptacles, or wires to which they will be connected.

Repairing Lamps

I f you lack patience, don't go into lamp repair. But if you like to take things apart to repair them, and you are patient enough to make note of where all the little pieces of the lamp should go when you are putting it back together, repairing lamps is actually quite a bit of fun. It involves a little wiring, a little problem solving, and a little mechanics; and it might just be an excuse to buy some new tools. You will usually find that lamps are held together by a center hollow rod that has a nut at the bottom. Once you undo that nut, the various lamp components will slide off the rod. The wire usually runs up the center of the rod, and that wire is what you are typically replacing in most repairs.

Replacing a Lamp Cord

tools and materials

- ◆ Insulated screwdriver
- ◆ Lamp cord
- ◆ Utility knife
- ◆ Wire stripper

1 Turn off the power. Pull the old cord through the center pipe and out through the lamp base.

2 Pull the new cord through the lamp base, and insert it into the socket base. Strip the ends of the wires.

3 Using an Underwriters' knot—see the Smart Tip on page 108—tie the wire ends; tuck them into the socket base; and connect the wires.

4 Attach the copper wire to the brass terminal and the silver wire to the silver terminal. Reassemble the socket.

Replacing a Light Socket and Switch

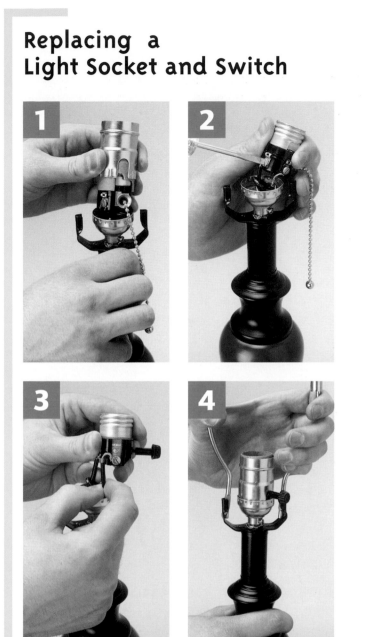

1 Squeeze the brass sleeve above the base cap, and slip off both the sleeve and the inside insulator (often cardboard).

2 Loosen the terminal screws; disconnect the wires; and remove the old switch.

3 Connect the hot wires to the new socket. The wires should fit snugly under the terminal screws; if not, then re-twist them.

4 Place the insulator and brass shell over the socket. Tighten the setscrew holding the cord in the socket, if there is one, and replace the harp.

Socket and Switch Anatomy

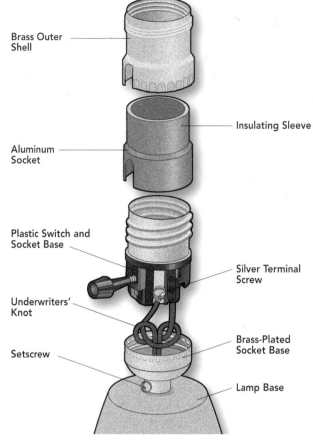

Brass Outer Shell

Insulating Sleeve

Aluminum Socket

Plastic Switch and Socket Base

Silver Terminal Screw

Underwriters' Knot

Brass-Plated Socket Base

Setscrew

Lamp Base

A lamp socket that has a built-in switch is illustrated above. If either the socket or the switch is faulty, it is best to replace them both; if the cord is damaged, then replace it, too.

SMART TIP

Before checking an old cord, be sure it is unplugged. Examine the wire carefully for cracking, fraying, and dryness. Replace all worn or damaged cords.

Wiring Safety Detectors

Most city and town building codes now require that every room have a working smoke detector. It's a good idea, and these devices have saved countless lives. Many smoke detectors can now be linked. So if one is triggered, it will activate the other detectors in the home. (That capability is hard to retrofit, so yours may not be linked.) Smoke detectors used to be just battery powered, but now they are hardwired, with battery backup. They are wired just as an outlet or switch is wired. The mounting screws on the smoke detector's chassis match up to the holes on the utility box.

1

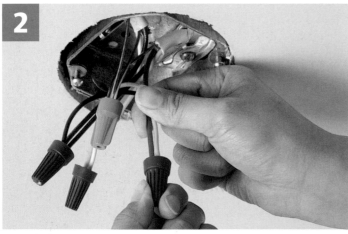

2

3

Hard-Wiring Smoke Detectors

tools and materials
- Flat-head screwdriver
- Needle-nose pliers
- Lineman's pliers
- Wire strippers
- 2- and 3-wire cables

1 In parallel, run two-wire cable into the first detector and three-wire cable between detectors.

2 Splice two-wire cable to the first smoke detector, and three-wire cable to the next detector. (See Smart Tip below.)

3 Wire the remaining detectors; plug in the wiring modules; and mount the detectors.

SMART TIP

Hardwired detectors have wiring modules that contain protruding wires to which you make your connections. In general, attach like-color wires together, but follow manufacturer's directions.

Wiring a Series of Smoke Detectors

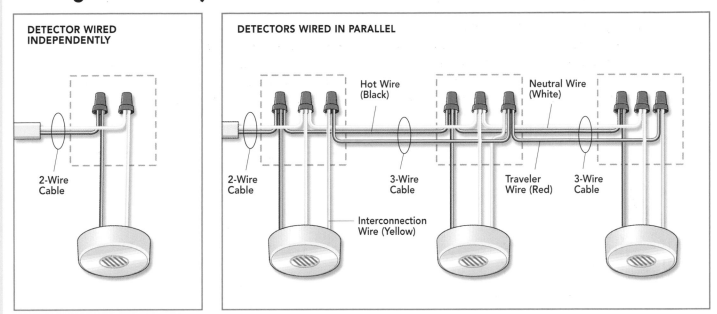

DETECTOR WIRED INDEPENDENTLY

2-Wire Cable

DETECTORS WIRED IN PARALLEL

Hot Wire (Black)

Neutral Wire (White)

2-Wire Cable

3-Wire Cable

Traveler Wire (Red)

3-Wire Cable

Interconnection Wire (Yellow)

Smoke detectors can be wired independently or in parallel. To wire in parallel, use a three-wire smoke detector. When one alarm sounds, they will all sound.

Hard-Wiring Carbon Monoxide (CO) Detectors

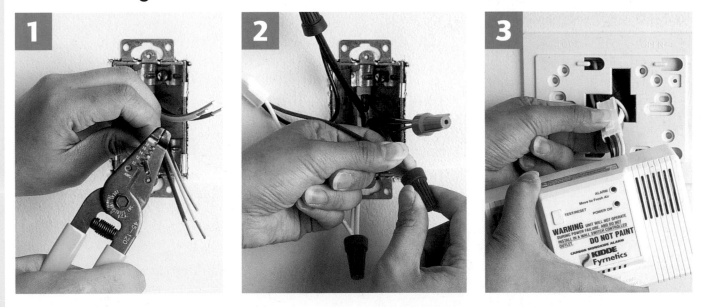

1 Locate the electrical boxes for carbon monoxide detectors on a wall or ceiling.

2 Using 14- or 12-gauge 2-wire cable, bring power into the first detector box from the main panel.

3 Wire the remaining detectors in parallel, using 3-wire cable.

Specialty Wiring

Some devices—such as timers and motion detectors—have very specific wiring requirements that are different from the typical wiring used to serve outlets and switches. Though it may seem daunting at first, study the wiring schematic that comes with the device you are trying to wire. The schematic is a map-like drawing that designates which wires go where. The schematic will often indicate the color of the wires, so it is easier than it looks to match the wires from your circuit to the wires of the specialty device.

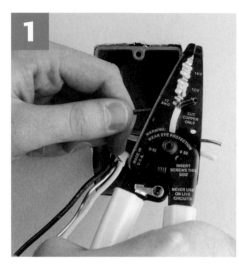

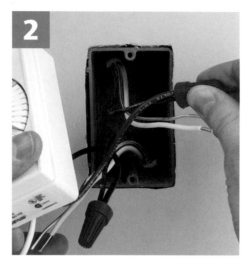

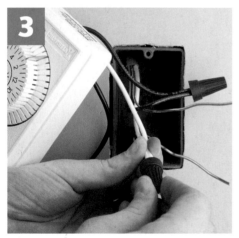

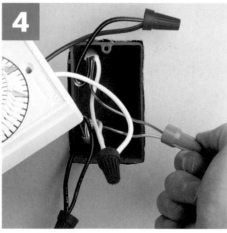

Wiring a Clock-Timer Switch

tools and materials

- Insulated screwdrivers
- Long-nose pliers
- Wire stripper
- Cable ripper
- Switch box
- Clock-timer switch
- Red and green wire
- No. 14/2g NM Cable connectors

1 Clock-timer switches require two cables—one from the power source and one from the controlled device.

2 Splice the hot wires from the switch to those from the power source and the device being controlled.

3 Splice the timer-switch neutral wire to the supply and device neutral wires inside the switch box.

4 Splice the grounding wires from the source and the fixture. If the box is metal, pigtail them to the box.

5 Carefully secure the wiring in the switch box; then mount the timer switch to the box.

SMART TIP

Don't discard the directions or the wiring schematic (the wire routing map) that comes in the box. Keep it on hand in case there is a problem at a later date. The wiring instructions are specific to your device

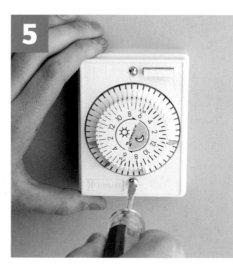

Replacing a Thermostat

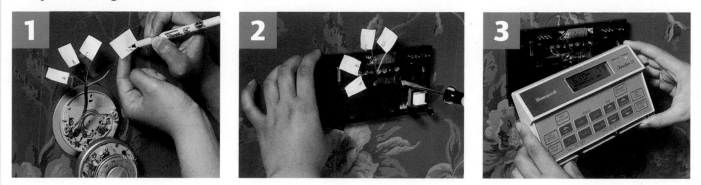

1 Loosen the old thermostat from its wall mount, and mark the terminal location and color of each wire you disconnect.

2 Mount the base of the new thermostat in the same location (away from heat sources), and pull through the tagged wires.

3 Remove the tags, and attach old wires to the new thermostat one at a time. Finish by installing the new faceplate.

Wiring a Monitor Sensor

Splice the hot, neutral, and grounding wires from the motion sensor to the corresponding circuit wires.

Secure the wiring, and attach the sensor box. Set and test the controls.

Wiring Other Types of Timers

A time-delay switch operates a device for a given period of time, as opposed to operating it at a specified time.

A digital timer switch is programmable, allowing you to set multiple on/off cycles during the day. Cycles may be set at either regular or random intervals.

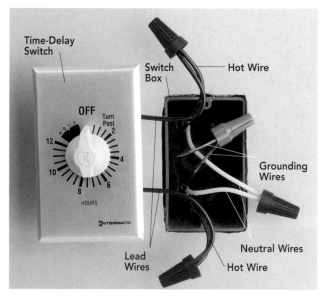

Telephone Wiring

Wiring telephones is easy. But it may look complicated because the wires are so small, and there are often four of them jacketed inside a phone cable. However, most phones work with just two wires, and they are low-voltage connections. The only real challenge is stripping the delicate copper wire leads in such a way that you don't cut the wire entirely. After you get the wires stripped, and you have them hooked up to the phone jack, it's easy to test the circuit: you just pick up the phone. It works or it doesn't. If it doesn't, you can start reworking the connections until you get dial tone.

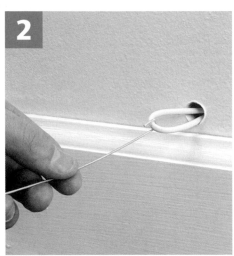

Wiring a Telephone Jack

tools and materials
◆ Flat-head screwdriver
◆ Needle-nose pliers
◆ Lineman's pliers
◆ Wire strippers ◆ Circuit tester
◆ Small screwdriver

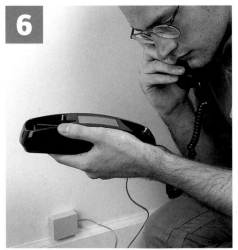

1 Connect station wires to screw terminals or a punch-down block in a telephone wire junction.

2 Fish the telephone cable through the wall to where the telephone jack will be mounted.

3 Pull telephone cable through a hole cut in the wall; rip the cable sheathing, and strip the telephone wires.

4 Mount the telephone jack; connect the lead (spade tip) wires to the jack; and attach the jack cover plate.

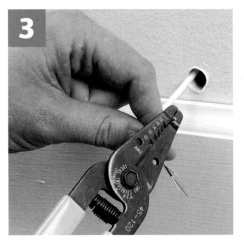

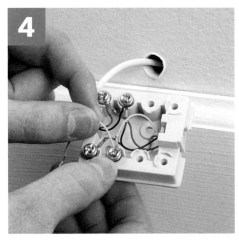

5 Using a telephone line tester, test the polarity of the telephone jack. A green light indicates correct wiring.

6 Plug a telephone receiver into the jack; then listen for a dial tone. If there's no tone, recheck the wiring.

SMART TIP

Although local telephone companies generally provide you with enough power to ring five telephones on a single line, the actual number you can install is determined by the amount of power required by the particular telephone—some phones require more power than others. The power required is represented by a number, called a ringer equivalency number (REN). The total number of telephones that you can install on your line is determined by adding up the RENs on your phones. If the number is less than five, you will not have any problems. If the number exceeds five, your phones will still work, but not all phones on the line will ring. Either reduce the number of phones on the line, or replace one or more with phones having a lower REN.

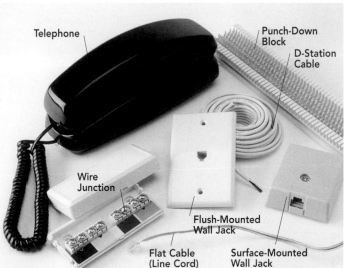

A **basic telephone system** consists of a service entrance, a wire junction, telephone station cable, a surface- or flush-mounted wall jack, flat cable, and a telephone.

Telephone Wiring Layouts

Telephone wiring can be run using either a home-run system, in which each telephone jack is directly wired to a wire junction, or a loop system, in which wiring runs from jack to jack in an open or closed loop that returns to the wire junction and provides a second wiring path. Up to three jacks may be wired to one wire junction.

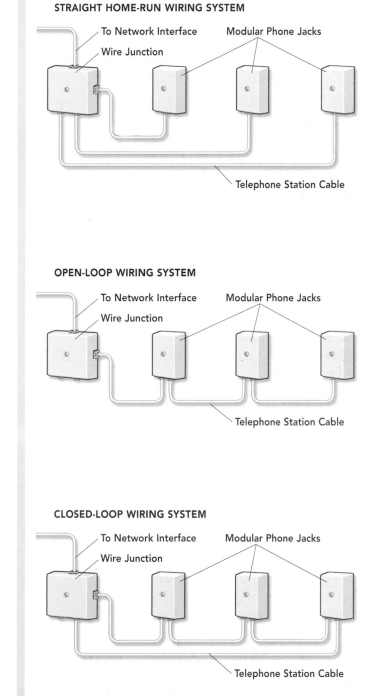

STRAIGHT HOME-RUN WIRING SYSTEM

To Network Interface Modular Phone Jacks
Wire Junction
Telephone Station Cable

OPEN-LOOP WIRING SYSTEM

To Network Interface Modular Phone Jacks
Wire Junction
Telephone Station Cable

CLOSED-LOOP WIRING SYSTEM

To Network Interface Modular Phone Jacks
Wire Junction
Telephone Station Cable

The Basics of Home Networking

A home networking system is a path for linking computers to one another and piping video and sound throughout the house. In a full-blown system, phone lines and cable connections are connected to a central hub in the house, similar to electrical wires connected to a breaker box. From the hub, the wiring—called structured cabling—is routed to structured cabling outlets. When installed, these outlets provide networking capability. For example, some outlets give you access to a high-speed Internet connection; others connect you to a cable TV system. We show some of the basic connections here.

Attaching a Plug to a Category 5 Cable

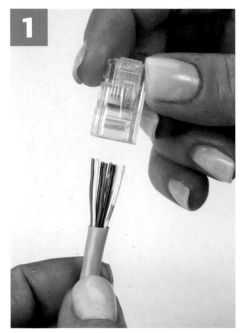

tools and materials

◆ Wire stripper
◆ RJ45 crimp tool
◆ Category 5 or 5e cable
◆ Modular plugs

1 Remove the outer insulation, and fan out the twisted pairs of wires. Follow the guide that comes with the plug to insert each wire in the correct channel.

2 There should be no exposed wires. Place the plug in the crimp tool, and squeeze the handles to attach the plug to the cable. Some tools have a blade for trimming wires.

Attaching an F-Connector to Coaxial Cable

tools and materials

◆ Coaxial cable cutter & stripper
◆ Utility knife (optional)
◆ F-connectors ◆ Crimping tool
◆ Coaxial cable

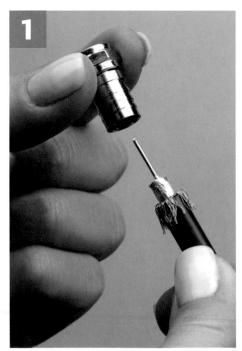

1 Use a coaxial-cable stripper to prepare the cable. The connector is threaded so that it can be attached to the threaded post of video equipment and computer modems.

2 The center conductor should extend about 1/16 in. beyond the end of the F-connector. Use a crimping tool to make the permanent connection.

Structured Cabling

Structured cabling systems rely primarily on two types of cabling. Coaxial cable carries video and data signals throughout the house. Category 5 cable transmits voice and data signals.

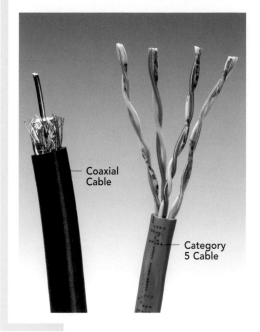

Coaxial Cable

Category 5 Cable

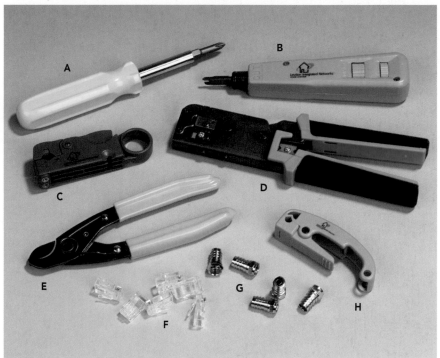

Structured cabling tools: A screwdriver; **B** punch-down tool; **C** coaxial-cable stripper; **D** RJ45 crimp tool; **E** wire cutter; **F** Cat-5 plugs; **G** F-connectors; **H** cable-crimp tool

SMART TIP

Installing structured cabling is similar to installing electrical cables and wires. But there are some differences.

✔ Do not bend the cable or nick the protective covering.

✔ Do not run structured cabling parallel with electrical wiring. If structured cables and electrical cables must cross, they should cross at a 90-degree angle.

✔ Structured cabling wall outlets should not share a stud with electrical outlets.

✔ Structured cabling should not share stud bore holes or conduit with electrical cables.

✔ Use plastic staples for securing cables. Cables should be loose under staples.

Connecting Cable to a Terminal Jack

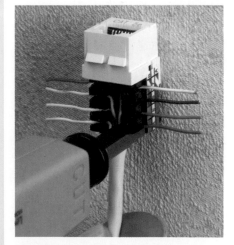

Use the punch-down tool to connect the conductors to the jack. Note the color coding on the jack.

7
Making Improvements

Improving Home Security

Though you might think of home security as burglar alarms and motion detectors, real security begins with much simpler items, such as reinforced doorjambs and locks that work as they should. Take the first steps to making your home more secure by making note of its weak points—window locks that don't work, entry doors without deadbolts, and the like. Once you have the little stuff out the way, consider installing a home alarm system. Some of the these systems are designed to do-it-yourself installation; however, only professionals can install and maintain truly advanced systems.

Strengthening Door Frames

tools and materials
- Pry bar ◆ Power drill/driver
- Shims ◆ Wood screws

1 Prevent kick-in entries where burglars crash in the door and jamb with the lock intact. First, remove the trim.

2 Insert blocks of wood at several points into the gaps between the door casing and the house wall framing.

3 Remove the stop or weather stripping so you can drive screws through the door casing and blocks into the house frame.

4 Use screws long enough to reach at least an inch into the nearest wall stud. Replace the stop to conceal screwheads.

Security System Components

There are a wide range of security devices available. At most home centers, you can buy motion detectors, door alarms, fire alarms, temperature sensors, and whole-house security systems. No security system would be complete without smoke and carbon monoxide protection.

WHOLE-HOUSE SECURITY SYSTEM

WINDOW SENSORS

Security System Layout

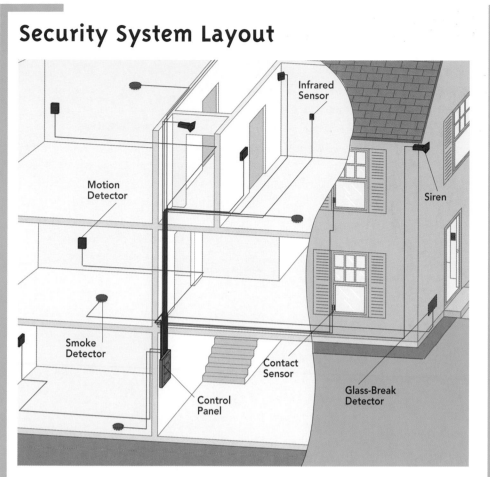

A complete home alarm system can combine many different security functions: monitoring entry at windows and doors, sensing motion inside rooms, and reacting to signals from a variety of sensors such as smoke alarms.

If you are going to pay for a sophisticated system, it makes sense that you bring in an expert to help you specify the coverage of the system because each house has different requirements. A good lock on the basement door and secure basement windows may save you the expense of wiring the entire room, while infrared detectors and motion detectors may have overlapping coverage that makes one of them unnecessary.

Security Hardware

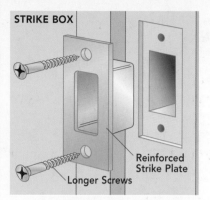

STRIKE BOX

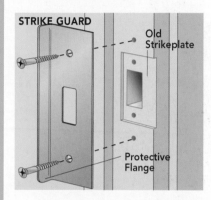

STRIKE GUARD

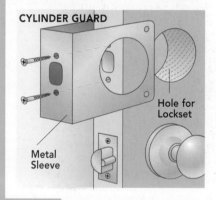

CYLINDER GUARD

DOOR SENSORS

REMOTE CONTROLS

AUDIO ALARMS

MOTION DETECTOR

Improving Home Safety

How many times have you head the expression, "An ounce of prevention is worth a pound of cure"? That sentiment is especially true in homes, where the cost of small efforts to make the surroundings safer is always a fraction off the cost incurred—financially and emotionally—when someone gets hurt. If you have ever "baby-proofed" or "senior-proofed" a home, you know that entire sections of home centers are dedicated to extraordinarily clever gadgets and devices that can make a home safer, including gates that can be held in place with simple friction to stop toddlers from climbing stairs. A Velcro strap or some small plastic clips can guard an entire cabinet full of cleaning supplies from Junior, and window grates can bring peace of mind when placed in playrooms or your child's bedroom. If you look around your house and try thinking like a kid, you'll see that there is no such thing as being too cautious.

Built-In Features

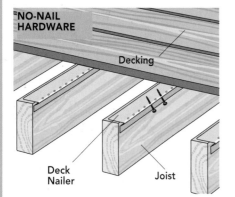

NO-NAIL HARDWARE

Decking

Deck Nailer

Joist

Avoid accidents on decks (raised nails) with hardware that allows you to fasten boards from below.

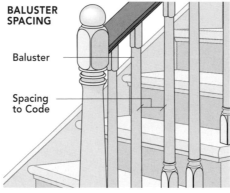

BALUSTER SPACING

Baluster

Spacing to Code

Codes control spacing (4 in. max) between parts of stairs and railings to avoid accidents.

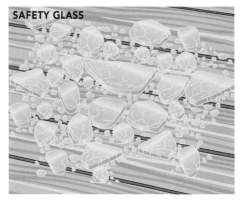

SAFETY GLASS

Standard glass breaks into razor-sharp shards, but tempered safety glass breaks into pebble-like pieces.

Openings

Safety grates can prevent falls. Building codes ban locks if the window is a fire-escape route.

Safety gates can keep toddlers off of stairs. This model has mesh panels that won't trap children.

Reduce the risk of accidents with land-scaping tools and materials by walling them off with a hinged lattice gate.

Soft Surfaces

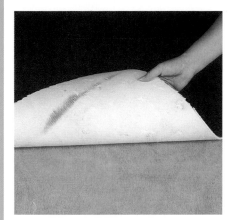

Reduce noise transmission and take the edge out of falls with wall-to-wall carpet over a thick pad.

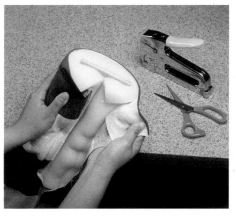

This cushioned chair rail for a child's room has thick foam stapled around a strip of fabric-padded plywood.

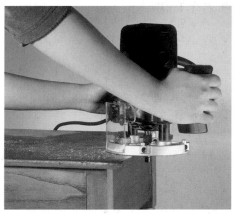

On furniture where you can't create cushioned surfaces, reduce hard edges with a roundover bit.

Hazardous Materials

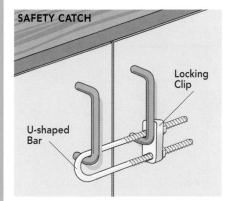

SAFETY CATCH

Locking Clip

U-shaped Bar

Remove all hazardous materials from children's reach or lock up the cabinets that contain them

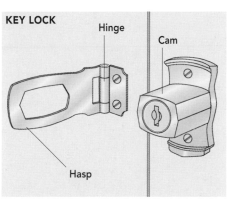

KEY LOCK

Hinge

Cam

Hasp

There are locks to fit every type of door, including hasp locks that can't be opened without a key.

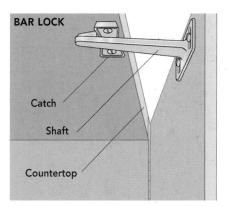

BAR LOCK

Catch

Shaft

Countertop

Where only minimal security is needed, this under-counter spring lock will keep a door from opening fully.

Electricity

Short cords are inconvenient on countertop appliances, but they keep the wires away from children.

Eliminate shock hazards on electrical outlets not in use by plugging a plastic insulator cap into the receptacle.

Often required by code, circuit-breaker outlets (ground-fault circuit interrupters) reduce shock hazard.

Testing for Lead in Water

Sources of lead in drinking water include lead pipes (common until around 1930), brass faucets or fittings that contain some lead, or copper pipes soldered with material containing lead. If you suspect there is lead in your water, have it tested. To reduce the lead you may be consuming if you're at risk, use cold water for consumption (it doesn't sit in pipes for long), and run the tap 1 or 2 minutes before you drink. You may have to replace old pipes.

To take a sample of water for testing, first use the flame from a match to burn off impurities on the faucet head.

Fill a small, clean container with a sample, which can be tested by some town health departments or private labs.

Testing for Radon

Radon (a colorless, odorless gas) is the second-leading cause of lung cancer after smoking. This naturally occurring gas comes from the ground, well water, and some building materials. Test your home with a canister kit you buy at home centers. Indoor levels of 4 picocuries per liter or more need to be fixed. Contractors can install an air-pumping system that vents radon from under your house to the outside as one possible solution.

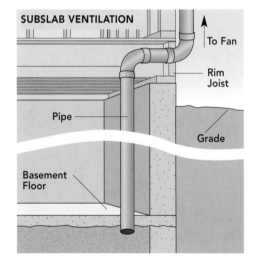

SUBSLAB VENTILATION

To Fan

Rim Joist

Pipe

Grade

Basement Floor

A radon test kit consists of a small canister that you leave in your living areas. You mail it to a lab for results.

Testing for a Gas Leak

A natural- or propane-gas leak is detectable due to mercaptan, an additive in gas that has a rotten-egg smell. If you suspect a gas leak, the safest course is to leave the house immediately and report it to 911 and the utility. If you suspect problems in a gas-fired appliance but don't smell the overwhelming aroma of a major leak, you can turn off the gas at the appliance or the main valve at the gas meter.

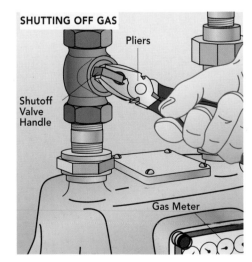

SHUTTING OFF GAS

Pliers

Shutoff Valve Handle

Gas Meter

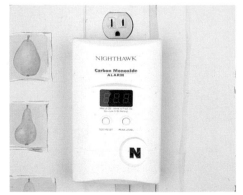

Specialized natural gas alarms can detect small amounts of leaking methane and propane in your home.

Fire Safety Checklist

- ✔ **Don't overload:** Do not plug more than one heat-producing device into an outlet.

- ✔ **Maintain smoke detector:** Replace battery twice a year; test a detector monthly; and replace it every 10 years.

- ✔ **Provide safe egress:** Have two ways out of every room—a door and a code-compliant egress window—including rooms in finished basements.

- ✔ **Fire-safe security:** Don't use security locks, bars, or devices that make it difficult to escape a fire.

- ✔ **Clean your chimney:** Have wood-burning chimneys inspected annually and cleaned as needed.

- ✔ **Store inflammables safely:** Store inflammable liquids in original containers with tight-fitting lids. Keep them away from heat and flames, preferably in a shed.

- ✔ **Be prepared:** Keep an extinguisher handy to stop a small fire from spreading. In other cases, call 911.

Fire Extinguishers

Most homes need at least two extinguishers: a small unit in the kitchen, and a larger, wall-mounted unit (generally installed in a closet) to use elsewhere. To avoid confusion in a fire emergency, choose A-B-C-rated units that work on all types of fires. To use an extinguisher effectively, remember the acronym P A S S—Pull (the pin), Aim, Squeeze, and Sweep.

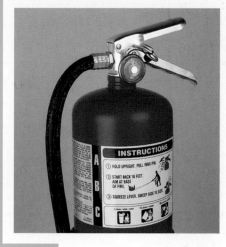

Use an all-purpose A-B-C extinguisher against paper, grease, and electrical fires. Aim at the base of the fire.

SMART TIP

Asbestos is often safe if sealed and contained on site. Removing it can make the dangerous particulates airborne, which is when they do real damage.

Dealing with Asbestos

Asbestos is often found as insulation and fire protection on pipes. It was also used in flooring and siding materials in houses built between 1930 and 1950. Loose asbestos fibers are hazardous. The safest course of action is to leave it undisturbed—asbestos in good shape won't release fibers. You can wrap undamaged sections. If asbestos needs to be removed, hire a licensed abatement contractor.

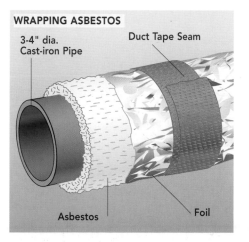

WRAPPING ASBESTOS

3-4" dia. Cast-iron Pipe

Duct Tape Seam

Asbestos

Foil

Asbestos is commonly found on pipes in older homes. Test a sample before deciding on removal.

Saving Energy

Energy will only get more expensive over time—that's a given. In many cases, older homes are inefficient because energy conversation wasn't a focus of the home builder or even the homeowner until recently. Now that energy prices are spiking, energy conversation has finally grabbed our attention. Many homeowners can improve the efficiency of their homes drastically with just a few basic, low-cost retrofit activities, such as adding more insulation in the attic and sealing the openings around windows and doors, which can lose a shocking amount of conditioned air. Once you've completed the easy stuff, you can always step up from the weekend projects of caulking and sealing to more serious activities like replacing drafty windows and doors with new ones that are far more efficient. At the rates energy costs are climbing, payback for most energy-saving upgrades is faster than you think.

The Thermal Envelope

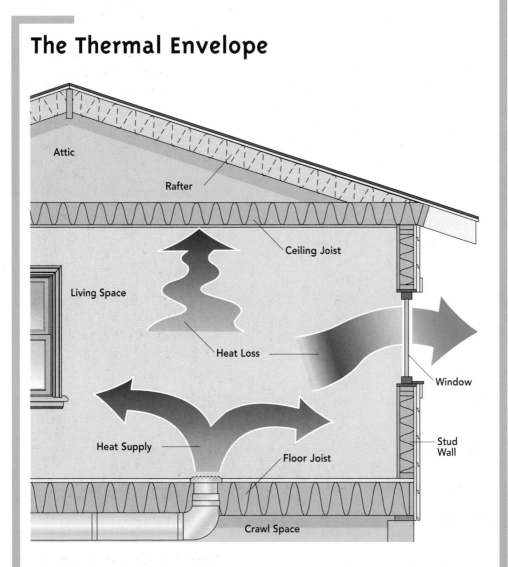

Heat moves toward colder surfaces and is conducted through walls and windows to the colder air outside. Insulation materials are poor conductors of heat—they slow the escape of warm air from your house.

Insulation Performance

The most common type of insulation is fiberglass. Its R-values range from R-11 to R-38, depending on thickness. Other types of materials include blown cellulose, foam boards, sprayed foams, and materials such as vermiculite and perlite.

The table below compares approximate R-values for different types of common insulation. Each material is evaluated on how much resistance to heat flow it offers. R-value means resistance to heat flow. Values can be slightly different for very similar materials.

Insulation Performance Ratings

FIBERGLASS BATTS

3½"	R-11
6½"	R-21
7"	R-23
9"	R-30
13"	R-43

LOOSE FILL (per inch)

Cellulose	R-3
Perlite	R-3
Vermiculite	R-2

RIGID BOARD (per inch)

Expanded Polystyrene	R-4
Dense Polystyrene	R-4
Extruded Polystyrene	R-5
Polyurethane	R-6
Polyisocyanurate	R-6–7

SPRAYED OR FOAMED FILL (per inch)

Cellulose	R-3–4.0
Polyurethane	R-5.5–6.5

Common Types of Insulation

Fiberglass

◆ **Fiberglass**

The most common of wall and ceiling insulation materials, fiberglass insulation is installed in 80 percent of new homes. R-values, available in a variety of different thicknesses, range from R-11 to R-38. Unfaced batts can be laid on top of themselves to create super-insulated attics. Most residential applications use either rolls or precut batts.

Mineral Wool

◆ **Mineral wool**

Like fiberglass, mineral wool is made from a hard mineral slag and spun into a soft material. Mineral wool gets clumpy when wet and will lose R-value. When dry, mineral wool has the same R-value as fiberglass.

Cellulose Loose Fill

◆ **Cellulose loose fill**

Cellulose is made from shredded newspapers that have been chemically treated with a fire retardant. It is sold in large bags and can be easily poured in between attic floor joists or professionally blown into wall cavities. When it is blown into walls, some settling can occur, creating under-insulated slices along the ceiling line.

Extruded Polystyrene

◆ **Extruded polystyrene**

This rigid form board has an R-value of about 5.0 per inch; it is a denser polystyrene than expanded polystyrene (Syrofoam) and pink or blue in color. Another product, expanded polystyrene (EPS), has many tiny foam beads pressed together, like a styrene foam coffee cup or cooler. EPS is commonly called "beadboard" and has an R-value of about 3.5 per inch of thickness.

Polyurethane

◆ **Polyurethane**

This versatile type of foam has a white or yellowish color and an R-value of about 6.0 per inch. Rigid panels can be faced with foil for radiant heat deflection. Used on a large scale on exposed framing, the material also can be mixed on site and sprayed into place as a dense liquid that fills both large areas and small spaces in irregular framing bays. The material bubbles up after application and is later trimmed flush with framing.

Polyisocyanurate

◆ **Polyisocyanurate**

This plastic has an R-value of approximately 6.0 per inch. It has a white or yellowish appearance and is usually backed with foil for radiant heat reflection.

Tools and Equipment

An advantage rigid board and foil bubble pack have over fiberglass is that they require no protection against airborne particles. You can easily cut rigid boards using a utility knife, and you don't need to wear gloves and a dust mask. With fiberglass insulation, however, you must take care to protect your eyes and lungs from glass fibers that can become lodged in your skin or breathed into your lungs. **WARNING:** If you encounter asbestos insulation on old pipes, do not attempt to remove it yourself—call in a professional.

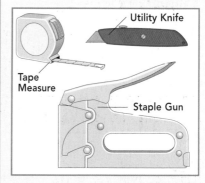

Most insulation is installed with simple tools that are probably already in your garage or workshop.

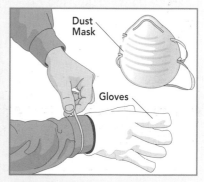

Protective gear includes gloves, dust mask, and a shirt with long sleeves secured with rubber bands.

Insulating Walls

tools and materials

- Staple gun
- Dust or respirator mask
- Work gloves
- Batt or blanket insulation
- Heavy-duty staples
- 6-mil polyethylene vapor barrier

1 Wear gloves and a long-sleeved shirt when you unroll fiberglass. Cut it to length using a sharp bread or paring knife.

2 Fit the batt between framing members by hand. You should wear a dust or respirator mask and gloves for protection.

Insulating Ceilings

tools and materials

- Utility knife
- Batt, blanket, or loose-fill insulation
- Plywood baffles

1 To avoid condensation due to trapped moisture, slit the facing of new batts or use unfaced blankets over existing insulation.

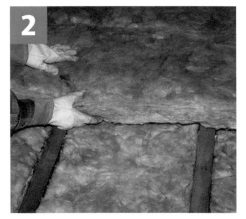

2 For maximum thermal effectiveness, run new insulation over both the old insulation and the framing members.

Insulating Roofs

tools and materials

- Staple gun
- Dust or respirator mask
- Work gloves
- Batt or blanket insulation
- Air baffles
- Heavy-duty staples
- 6-mil polyethylene vapor barrier

1 Staple air-chamber baffles to the underside of the roof sheathing before installing batts between rafters.

2 Because air can circulate through the baffles, you can fill the remaining space between rafters with batts.

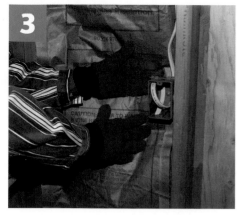

3 Run the insulation behind pipes, outlet boxes, and other obstacles to reduce thermal loss and prevent pipe freezing.

4 Flatten out the flanges extending from each side of the batt, and then staple them to the wall studs.

3 Loose fill is poured into the spaces between joists. Keep it a few inches away from obstructions, such as recessed lights.

4 Install plywood baffles above exterior walls to prevent loose fill from blocking vents in the roof overhang.

3 Position and flatten the insulation the same way you would between wall studs. Batts should not compress the air baffles.

4 Trim and fit insulation in irregular openings and around obstructions to create a complete thermal barrier.

SMART TIP

For maximum protection against fiberglass insulation, seal the gap between your gloves and a long-sleeve shirt with masking tape, to keep the fibers out.

Keep Insulation Away from Recessed Lights

Keep loose fill in ceilings away from recessed light fixtures, which need air flow to prevent overheating, unless the fixtures are rated for insulation contact. For those fixtures that are not rated for insulation contact, keep insulation at least 3 inches away from the fixture. Also keep loose fill in attics away from eaves vents. Install some form of dam above the exterior stud wall to hold back the loose fill.

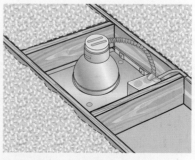

Keep loose insulation away from recessed ceiling light fixtures. Heat from the lamp could start a fire.

Insulating a Crawl Space

tools and materials
- ◆ Staple gun ◆ Work gloves
- ◆ Dust or respirator mask
- ◆ Batt or blanket insulation
- ◆ Heavy-duty staples ◆ Wire mesh

1 Batts of fiberglass insulation should be installed in the bays between the floor joists.

2 Staple wire mesh onto the joists, to keep out animals and prevent the insulation from sagging.

3 Staple fiberglass insulation batts onto knee walls above foundations. You can let the batts drape down over the masonry.

8 Weekend Projects to Conserve Energy

Caulk Windows and Doors
To stop air and water infiltration on the outside, apply a bead of flexible caulking, such as silicone, to exterior seams around all windows and doors.

Seal Holes
Foam expands like shaving cream out of its can and can be messy to work with if it's not contained in a hole or crevice. But foam is a good choice for where pipes go into walls.

Wrap Ducts
Ducts can be wrapped in paper-backed fiberglass insulation or foam-type material. Where ducts enter and exit through walls, ceilings, and roofs, seal the edges with foam insulation.

Close Gaps
Windows are often a major source of thermal loss. If you can feel a draft, remove the casing and stuff pieces of fiberglass insulation in any cracks between the window jambs and the framing.

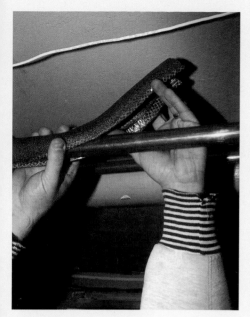

Wrap Pipes

To insulate pipes, buy preformed pipe sleeves that fit over the pipe, or wrap the pipe in thin fiberglass strips and secure them with duct tape. Both will prevent pipe sweating in the summer.

Encase Water Heater

A water heater can be wrapped in a fiberglass thermal blanket to cut down heat loss. Water-heater blankets are sold in kits that include tape and a thermal blanket encased in a plastic sleeve.

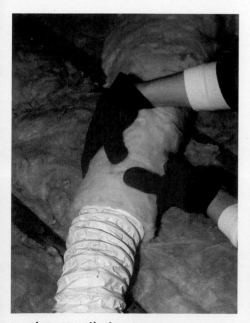

Insulate Ventilation Ducts

Wrap attic ventilation ducts with thin batts of fiberglass insulation. This insulation prevents condensation from forming—and then leaking down through the ceiling—where hot vented vapor meets cold attic air.

Seal Utility Boxes

An insulating pad inserted between a switch or receptacle and its cover will stop airflow. You can also inject silicone caulk around the box between the drywall or plaster if there are gaps.

Vapor Barriers

Vapor barriers block both air and water vapor. The only impervious barrier is foil. But you need to install foil-faced batts carefully, and tape the seams for maximum effect. Plastic sheeting is second best and often used over paper-faced batts to improve moisture resistance. Clear polyethylene sheets 6 mils thick are standard. All vapor barriers are rated by permeance (the ability of air to penetrate). To be reasonably effective, the perm rating should be less than 1. Polyethylene sheets have a perm rating of 0.04 to 0.08.

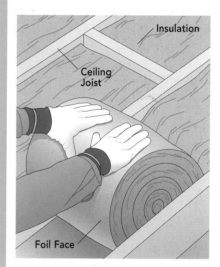

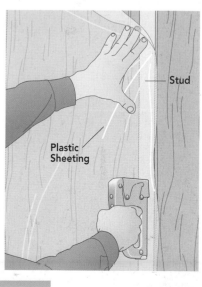

Adding Shelving

Even beginner carpenters can put up shelving that makes it look as though it were installed by a pro. The system shown below provides a good base for the metal standards that will support the shelving. But some systems attach directly to the wall; others rely on different methods of attachment. For most all you need are basic carpentry tools—level, drill, and tape measure—to install most shelving. One tool that will make the work go faster is a stud finder because shelving should be attached directly to wall studs.

Installing Shelving Standards

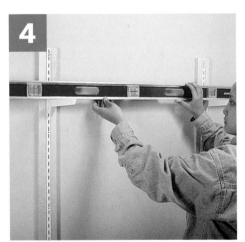

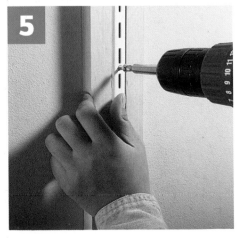

tools and materials

- Table saw, circular saw, or router
- Power drill/driver
- 4-ft. level ◆ Screws
- Measuring tape
- Eye protection
- 1x4 lumber for frame
- Metal shelf standards
- Shelf brackets
- Boards for shelving

1 Use a table saw to cut a groove down the center of the ¾-in. standard frame. A local lumberyard may make this cut for you.

2 Predrill in the grooves so that you can screw the frames to wall studs.

3 Center the standard frames on wall studs, level the bases, plumb them with a level, and screw them to the wall.

4 Seat each standard in its groove, and tack it with a screw. Temporarily mount two standards, and double-check for level.

5 Once the slots are dead level, drive the rest of the screws. The standard should sit flush with the surrounding wood.

6 Fit shelf brackets into corresponding slots in the standards, adjust spacing to suit, and mount the shelves.

Closet Systems

There are many types of closet systems. One of the most versatile is wire racks. Mix-and-match components include several stock lengths of shelving with integral hanging bars, plus support brackets and clips that allow you to install these systems in almost any configuration. They also are easy to alter. You can create the same kind of compartmentalized storage with custom and stock wood systems, or hire one of many specialized closet companies to help organize your belongings and build your system.

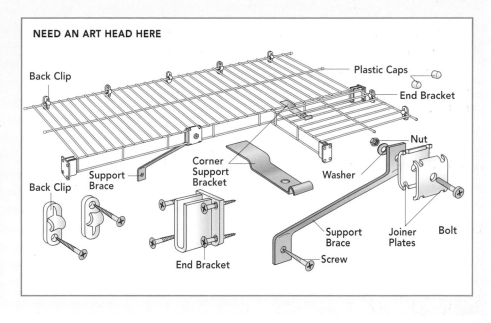

NEED AN ART HEAD HERE

Back Clip · Plastic Caps · End Bracket · Corner Support Bracket · Nut · Washer · Back Clip · Support Brace · Support Brace · Joiner Plates · Bolt · End Bracket · Screw

Standards

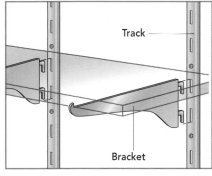

Track · Bracket

Slotted metal standards are leveled and screwed to wall studs. Shelf support brackets clip into the slots.

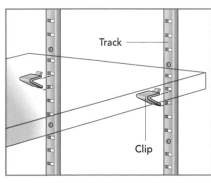

Track · Clip

Adjustable end-clip standards can be surface-mounted on side panels or screwed into side-panel grooves.

Closet systems include wood and laminate systems, top, and wire systems, bottom.

Shelving Materials

PINE

HARDWOOD

PLYWOOD

COMPOSITE

GLASS

Installing a Window Air Conditioner

Window air conditioners are a great way to deliver cool air where you need it. The hardest part is buying the right-size unit. Capacity is measured in Btu per hour, Btuh, which indicates the amount of heat energy the unit can remove from the air in one hour. As a general rule of thumb, a 12,000-Btu unit is a good size for a 500-square-foot room, but there is more that goes into calculating need. For help, go to www.energystar.gov to find the right-size unit for you.

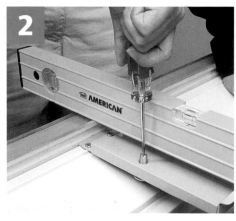

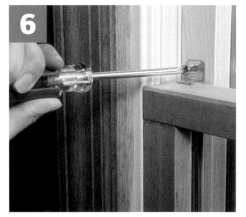

Installing a Window Unit

tools and materials

- ◆ Pencil
- ◆ Measuring tape
- ◆ Level
- ◆ Screwdriver or power drill/driver
- ◆ Caulking gun
- ◆ Window AC unit
- ◆ Waterproof caulk

1 Older units (and some very large machines) rest on external brackets, but modern ACs rest on a sill-mounted support.

2 One end of this bracket is screwed to the sill. You adjust a center screw to level the unit and provide condensation drainage.

3 This self-contained AC unit has integral handles that make it easier to set in position on the sill over the mounting bracket.

4 As you slide the machine into the window opening, a pocket underneath the machine locks in place over the bracket.

5 Extensions on both sides of the unit slide out to make a snug fit in the opening. Screw each extension to the sash.

6 Use the angle bracket provided with most machines to secure the two window sashes to each other over the AC unit.

SMART TIP

AC units cool the air and reduce humidity. Units that are too large will cool down a space quickly but will shut off before it can remove excess moisture in the air. The result is a cool, but clammy, room.

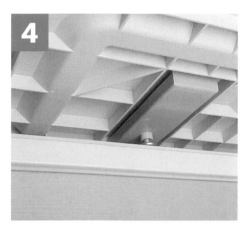

7 To seal the installation inside, use a foam strip (provided with most machines) to seal the air gap where the sash overlaps.

8 Caulk the unit outside, check the manufacturer's instructions for operation and maintenance, and plug in the unit.

Efficiency Rating Guide

You can compare air conditioners by checking their Energy Guide labels. These stickers explain annual electrical costs, compare efficiency among several units, and list an Energy Efficiency Rating (EER) number—a Seasonal Energy Efficiency Rating (SEER) on central air systems. This rating is the ratio of Btu used per hour of cooling to the watts used to produce those cooling Btu—fewer watts per Btu mean greater efficiency.

SEER

RATING	RECOMMENDATION
less than 9.7	old unit; replace with newer model
9.7/10	nat'l min. standard for single package/split-systems
12	recommended min. (Dept. of Energy)
18-plus	most efficient unit available

EER

RATING	RECOMMENDATION
less than 8	old unit; replace
8	nat'l min. standard
9.2	recommended min. for all units (but see below)
10	recommended min. for louvered unit 6000–19,999 Btuh
10–11.7	most efficient available

Window Fittings

If you install a window unit improperly, it may fall from the window when you raise the sash, damaging the unit and whatever happens to be underneath it. Install all brackets with the hardware provided; if the wood of your sills seems soft and partly rotten, use another window or replace the sill. If your windows have metal sashes instead of wood, use sheet-metal screws to install them.

For through-the-wall systems install caulk to seal the seams between the chassis and the siding.

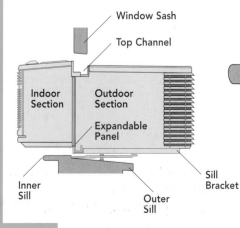

Window Sash
Top Channel
Indoor Section
Outdoor Section
Expandable Panel
Inner Sill
Outer Sill
Sill Bracket

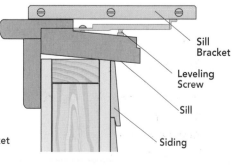

Sill Bracket
Leveling Screw
Sill
Siding

Adding Baseboard Molding

Nothing trims out a house more than molding. Adding molding, or trimwork, can add an elegant symmetry that is enormously pleasing to the eye. But trim carpentry can be extremely frustrating. The walls and ceilings in most homes are not completely flat; most corners do not form true 90-degree angles. All of those imperfections lead to small gaps when you try to form a seamless joint. So trimwork isn't only about doing the work; it is also about revising the work to get a perfect fit. One tip: rent a pneumatic nail gun to cut down on surface damage and the need to drill pilot holes.

Installing Baseboard Outside Corners

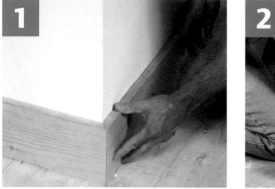

tools and materials

- ◆ Hammer ◆ Nail set
- ◆ Nail gun and nails (optional)
- ◆ Power miter saw
- ◆ Baseboard molding
- ◆ 4d finishing nails ◆ Glue
- ◆ Masking or painter's tape
- ◆ Shim stock

1 Test the angle of outside corners with two pieces of scrap 1x6 boards. Use a miter saw to cut a 45-deg. bevel on each piece, and hold them together around the corner.

2 Place masking tape strips on the floor around the corner; then hold a long piece of baseboard in place to mark it for cutting. Use these lines to mark the long point of each miter. (The shims shown here simulate the height of a finished floor.)

3 For an outside corner, cut and test the fit of the joint before nailing either piece in place. When you are satisfied with the joint, nail the first piece of baseboard to the wall.

4 Apply glue to the surfaces of the miter joint, and place the second piece in position. Make sure that the joint comes together tightly before nailing it to the wall. Use 4d finishing nails or brads to pin the joint together.

Corner Blocks

Corner blocks can add some remarkable distinction to otherwise boring baseboards, and all you have to do to install them is plan ahead. The baseboard has to be cut short to accommodate the corner board, so you have to decide the size of your corner blocks with real precision. The corner block can be any size, though it should be larger than your baseboard for the sake of proportion. That said, an oversized corner board can look grotesque, even comic. The best thing to do is to cut all the pieces for your baseboard and corner boards and assemble them in place.

Installing Inside Corner Baseboards

tools and materials
- Hammer ◆ Nail set
- Nail gun and nails (optional)
- Power miter saw ◆ Files or rasps
- Baseboard molding
- Finishing nails ◆ Shim stock

1 At inside corners, cut a square end on the first piece of baseboard and run it into the drywall corner. Because only the top portion of the molding will be visible, it does not need to be tight along its entire height. Note the use of a piece of finished flooring and cardboard as a spacer beneath the baseboard.

2 Cope the end of the second piece for an inside corner joint. (See page 142 for directions on how to create a coped joint.) Test the fit. If it's off, the wall may not be flat or straight, there's debris behind the molding, or your saw work needs polishing. Use a knife, rasp, file, or sandpaper to trim the boards to fit.

3 Completed inside corner joint on one-piece baseboard. It is not unusual for a joint to require some modification to close tightly.

Making the Cut

STANDARD MITER SAW

Installing molding involves making angled cuts in the wood to form seamless joints, especially at corners. A cut across the face of a board is called a miter; a bevel cut runs through the thickness of a board. Some joints require both a miter and a bevel for the same joint—these are called compound miters. The tools available can help make these cuts. In general, the angle that you cut on each half of a joint is equal to one-half of the total angle of the joint. So if the total angle is 90 degrees, each part needs to be cut a 45-degree angle. You can use the miter box, miter saw, or sliding compound miter saw to make miter and bevel cuts. There are differences among the tools, but the basics are the same: position the wood against the saw's fence, and align the cut line with the saw blade to make the cut. The coping saw is a flexible tool that allows you to follow the contours of a piece of molding.

MITER BOX

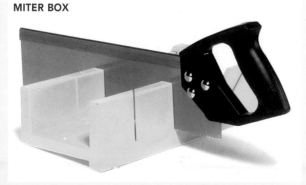

COPING SAW

SLIDING COMPOUND MITER SAW

Molding for Windows and Doors

The most common trim installation—and the easiest to get right, because they are mostly 45- and 90-degree angles—is the trim around windows and doors. There are a few tricks of the trade for installing this trim, and we've illustrated them below. As with most trim work, it is good to cut and assemble the trim pieces in place before you start to permanently nail them. That said, many a new carpenter has rushed in, nailed up some trim boards, and then found he or she had to remove them because of a mistake. That's OK Because trim is attached with finishing nails—the ones with a very thin head—it is fairly easy to remove trim to fix errors. You will just end up filling some nailholes.

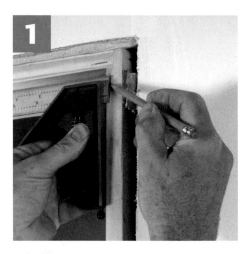

SMART TIP

If you are trying to remove a finishing nail, don't use a claw hammer to withdraw it. Instead, use pliers and pull it the rest of the way through the board. That leaves less of a mark on the wood.

Installing Simple Colonial Casing

tools and materials

- ◆ Hammer
- ◆ Combination square
- ◆ Power miter saw
- ◆ Nail set
- ◆ Clamshell or ranch casing
- ◆ Finishing nails
- ◆ Wood glue

1 Mark the reveal by sliding the blade on the combination square. A reveal is a ⅛-in. setback on the door jamb. Cut a miter on one end of the casing.

2 Align the short side of the miter with one reveal mark; transfer the opposite mark to the casing.

3 Use 4d finishing nails to tack the head casing to the head jamb of the door. Leave the nailheads exposed.

4 Cut a miter on a piece of side casing. Rest the miter on the floor or spacer (for carpet or finished floor).

5 Mark the length of the side casing pieces by running a pencil along the top edge of the head casing. Cut and install the casing.

Installing Corner Blocks

Interested in getting a little fancy with your door and window frames? Corner blocks are an easy way to make the trim work look as though it were installed by a pro. There is a fairly wide variety of corner block types, from blank square to Victorian fancy. So shop around and make sure your corner blocks are consistent with the theme of the trim elsewhere in the room and in your house.

Tack the rosette blocks in place, resting on the top of the side casings. Leave the nailheads exposed to make adjustment easier.

Fit the head casing between the rosette blocks. You may have to slightly adjust the relative position of casing and blocks to achieve tight joints.

Installing Window and Door Casing

BUTTED CASING WITH MITERED BACKBAND

BUTTED CASING WITH REVEAL

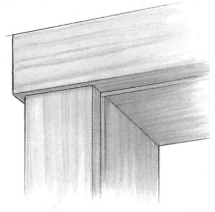

MITERED CASING

CASING WITH CORNER BLOCKS

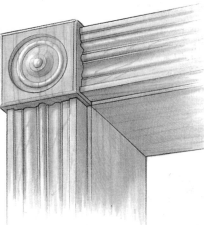

The first step to installing casing is establishing the reveal: the narrow strip of jamb that is left exposed when the casing is installed. Without a reveal, it will look as if you're trying to make the jamb and casing appear as one piece, but unsuccessfully. Most reveals are about ⅛ inch. When you decide what looks best, make light pencil marks representing the reveal on each jamb at the corners of the opening; use these marks for your measurements.

To install mitered casing, cut the casing pieces and temporarily tack them in place then make sure the joints fit tightly before permanently attaching the casing. Nail the casing to the jamb edges with small (4d or so) finishing nails; then nail through the outer edges of the casing into the wall framing, using 6d finishing nails.

If you're using corner and plinth blocks, install them first, then cut the casing to fit in between. It usually looks best if the casing is slightly narrower than the blocks, creating reveals on those pieces as well as along the jambs. Be sure you match the reveal from door casing to door casing, and window casing to window casing throughout the room, and even throughout the house. Consistency is key.

Cornice and Ceiling Molding

Now you're playing with the big dogs if you are taking on cornice and crown molding. It's fun work, but unforgiving of even small errors, so take your time, use sharp tools, and have some extra wood on hand for those inevitable times when you will make a mistake in your miter and coping saw cuts. What is especially rewarding about installing this kind of trim is how great it looks and how much you saved from not having to pay a carpenter to nail these boards to your wall. Cornice and ceiling molding comes in a variety of profiles, so before you install your trim, you may want to experiment with various styles to see which one looks best in your room.

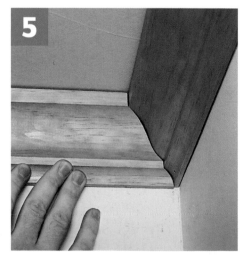

Installing Crown Molding

tools and materials

- ◆ Chalk-line box & measuring tape
- ◆ Crown molding & nailing blocks
- ◆ Power miter saw & coping saw
- ◆ Files ◆ Power drill & bits
- ◆ Hammer ◆ Finishing nails
- ◆ Nail set ◆ Wood glue
- ◆ Caulk & caulking gun

1 To get the results shown in photo 5, where the profile of one piece fits over the profile of another in a corner, make a coped joint. Use a coping saw to start the profile cut. Angle the saw to back-cut the coped piece.

2 Rotate the saw as needed to maneuver the thin blade along the profile of the miter.

3 Use an oval-shaped file (or a round file in tight spots) to clean up curved sections of the profile.

4 Use a flat rasp as needed to clean up the upper section of the coped cut or to increase the back-cut angle.

5 Test-fit the coped piece in place, supporting the other end to be sure the board is level.

SMART TIP

A good solid work surface where you can clamp the wood you are working on is essential to crisp, clean saw cuts.

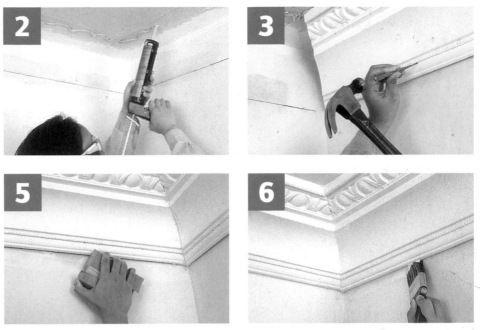

Installing Plastic Molded Cornice Trim

tools and materials

- ◆ **Power miter saw or backsaw & miter box**
- ◆ **Pencil** ◆ **Caulking gun**
- ◆ **Hammer** ◆ **Drywall taping knife**
- ◆ **Paintbrush** ◆ **Plastic Molded trim**
- ◆ **Construction adhesive**
- ◆ **Finishing nails** ◆ **Sandpaper**
- ◆ **Primer and paint**

1 Hold a section of the molded trim in place, and mark guidelines along the top and bottom edges with a pencil.

2 Following manufacturer's directions, install a bead of adhesive just inside your lines on the wall and ceiling.

3 Press the molding into the beads of adhesive, and fasten the lightweight sections with finishing nails.

4 Where molding sections meet, and along the top and bottom edges, use drywall compound to fill seams and gaps.

5 Spread the compound smoothly, and when it dries, lightly sand the wall and ceiling seams with fine sandpaper.

6 Wipe away sanding dust, cover the fresh compound primer and paint.

Installing a Medallion

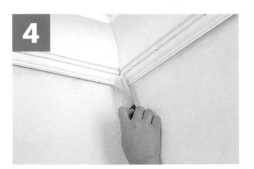

Apply a bead of adhesive specified by the manufacturer. Most replica medallions are lightweight foam.

For extra holding power, also drive a few finishing nails. Set the heads, and cover them with compound.

Touch up as needed to cover nail-heads. You can also paint medallions to blend in with the ceiling.

Paneling and Wainscoting

Concealing Nails

Cut the miter angles on both halves of an outside corner joint to test the fit before nailing the first piece to the wall. After you have the outside joints fit to your liking, nail the pieces into place. If you are not using a pneumatic finishing nailing gun (which countersinks the nails automatically), use a nail punch to countersink the nails. That means driving the nails just beneath the surface, so you or your painter can follow with wood filler to hide where the nail resides.

Installing Sheet Paneling

tools and materials

- ◆ Saber saw or keyhole saw ◆ 4-ft. level
- ◆ Hammer ◆ Measuring tape
- ◆ Straightedge ◆ Caulking gun
- ◆ Sheet paneling ◆ Caulk
- ◆ Finishing or ring-shanked nails
- ◆ Prefinished trim as required

1 Butt one end of the first sheet into a corner; then adjust the other end against a level so that the sheet is plumb.

2 Measure the height and width of utility boxes for cutouts. Precut them with a saber saw or keyhole saw.

3 Using a caulking gun, apply a bead of construction adhesive in a zig-zag pattern along the length of each stud face.

4 Nail the panel into place with paneling nails. Special ring-shanked nails are available in colors to match the paneling.

5 For a coordinated look, nail prefinished matching molding along the base and around windows and doors.

Installing Wainscoting

1 Walls need to be furred out with furring strips to ensure an even nailing surface. Shim any low spots.

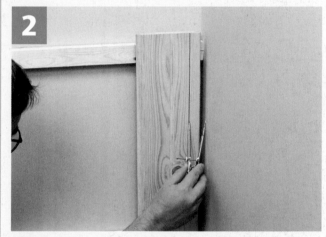

2 After the furring is completed, nail the first board into place. Scribe and cut its edge if the adjacent wall is not plumb.

3 Boards will have lapped edges or tongue-and-groove slot fittings. Attach boards to the furring with finishing nails.

Vinyl Flooring

Installing vinyl floors has been the inspiration for many slapstick comedies because some installations involve unwieldy rolls of material and glue—you get the picture. But a little advanced planning will help you install even sheet flooring right. For a less ambitious project, redo your floors with vinyl tiles. Some tiles have a peel-and-stick feature. We show the type of tiles that require a separate adhesive, generally considered the more superior installation. In either case, once you have the layout worked out, you can start installing the tiles easily. Vinyl tiles are easier to install than ceramic or natural stone for two reasons: there are not grout joints to fill between tiles; and you can cut vinyl using a sharp utility knife.

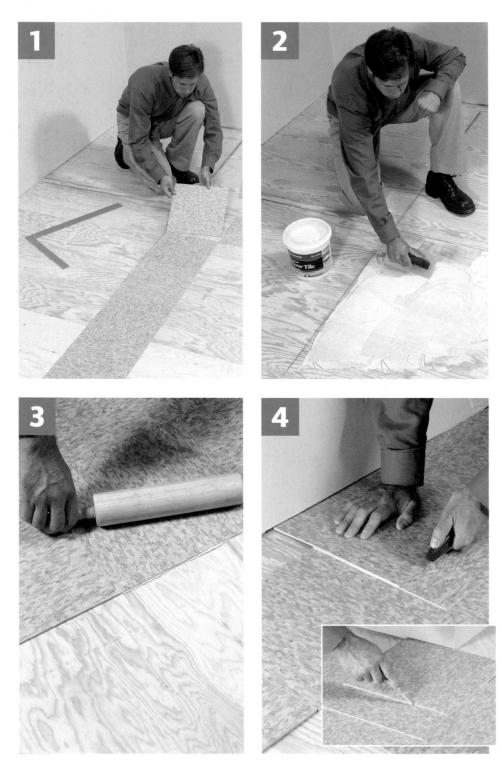

Installing Vinyl Floor Tile

tools and materials

◆ Framing square ◆ Chalk-line box
◆ Tape measure ◆ Utility knife
◆ Rolling pin or floor roller
◆ Resilient tiles ◆ Adhesive
◆ Solvent ◆ Notched trowel

1 After marking work lines on the floor, lay out the tiles dry to make sure your installation plans will work. Place the tiles against the work lines in all four directions.

2 Check the adhesive dry time, and work an area that you can finish in that time. Spread adhesive with a notched trowel held at a 45-deg. angle.

3 Lower tiles into place and press the tile down with your hands; then roll it smooth with a kitchen rolling pin or floor roller. If any adhesive squeezes up between tiles, wipe it up.

4 To cut a border tile, place a new full tile over the last full tile that has been installed. Then take another full tile and butt it against the wall. Cut along the edge of the top tile that's farthest away from the wall. To cut tiles for outside corners (inset), do the same thing, but on both sides of the corner.

Creating Layout Lines

When installing any type of tile floor, it is best to create layout lines to guide the installation. For a standard layout, snap chalk lines in the middle of opposite walls.

To create diagonal layout lines, measure out an equal distance along any two of the original perpendicular lines, and drive a nail at these points, marked A and B in the drawing. Hook the end of a measuring tape to each of the nails, and hold a pencil against the tape at a distance equal to that between the nails and the center point. Use the tape and pencil as a compass to scribe two sets of arcs on the floor. The arcs will intersect at point C.

Snap a diagonal line between the center and point C, extending the lines in each direction. Repeat the process for the other corners.

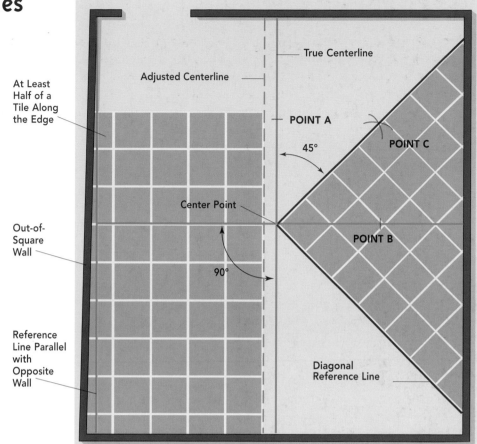

Tips for Installing Vinyl Sheet Flooring

Installing vinyl sheet flooring means using large rolls of material. If you can find a big open place to work, the job will be easier. Many people use the garage floor. Before you begin, create a scale drawing of the room on a piece of graph paper showing the exact outline of the flooring. A day before you begin, cut the roll to approximate size, and put the cut section in the room where it will be installed to acclimate it to temperature and humidity.

1 To fit inside corners, cut diagonally through the sheet margin until you can get the vinyl to lie flat.

2 To trim vinyl, use a framing square to guide your cut. Leave a ⅛-in. wide gap at the wall.

3 Use a rented floor roller to force out air bubbles. Work out from the center of the room toward the edges.

Laminate Flooring

Laminate flooring is relatively easy to install because the pieces rely on a tongue-and-groove design where one piece fits into the next. These are called floating floors because they are not attached to the subfloor in any way, making them a great remodeling project. The flooring is protected by the same type of material that protects laminate countertops, but it is much stronger. Most laminate floors come with a minimum warranty of 20 years. In most cases, there is no need to remove the existing floor, unless it is carpeting. Simply make sure the surface is clean without protruding nails or screws. Cover the old floor with the foam specified by the manufacturer and start flooring.

Installing Laminate Flooring

tools and materials
- ◆ **Laminate flooring** ◆ **Spacers** ◆ **Glue** ◆ **Hammer**
- ◆ **Plastic putty knife** ◆ **Foam underlayment padding**
- ◆ **Strap clamps** ◆ **Installation block**
- ◆ **Circular saw or handsaw** ◆ **Chalk-line box**

1 Make sure the existing flooring is in sound condition; then roll out the foam padding starting at one corner. If you are covering a concrete slab, most manufacturers require you to lay a polyethylene vapor barrier underneath the foam.

2 Assemble the first two or three rows of boards by spreading glue along the tongues (inset) and pushing the boards together. Install plastic spacers between the boards and the edges of the floor. The gaps created by these spacers give the floor room to expand with changes in temperature and humidity without buckling.

3 If you can't push a board in place using only your hands, then gently drive the boards together using a soft wood block. Don't strike the block too hard because this might cause damage to the tongue on the board. Remove any excess glue using a plastic putty knife.

4 After you've installed three or four rows of boards, hold them with strap clamps, and let the glue set up for about an hour before continuing. As you progress across the floor, just lengthen the clamp straps.

5 To measure the perimeter boards that need cutting, first lay a full plank over the last installed board. Use a third board, pushed against the wall, to scribe the board that needs cutting. Make the cut using a circular saw and a fine-tooth blade.

The Layers of Laminate

Laminate flooring has two things going for it: it is easy to install, and it can be made to look like anything, including wood, stone, ceramic tile, or any color of the rainbow. The inner fiberboard core provides dimensional stability and water resistance that make these products suitable for installation in a kitchen; the wear layers protect a decorative image. You can install laminate flooring over any substrate except carpeting. Simply make sure that the original flooring is clean and level. Most manufacturers require a foam padding under the floor. A glue-type installation is shown opposite, but some manufacturers also offer a glueless version where the individual components snap together.

SMART TIP

If installing a glue-type floor, be sure to use clamps to hold the sections together until the glue sets up. If you don't, gaps will form between planks.

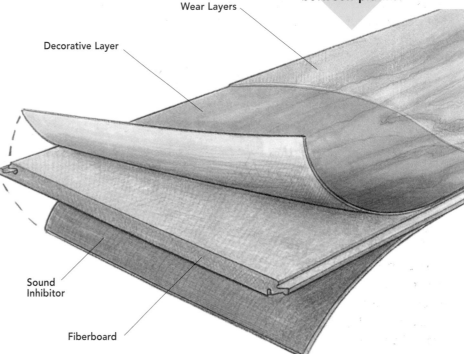

Wear Layers

Decorative Layer

Sound Inhibitor

Fiberboard

3

4

5

Kit Furniture

Kit furniture is very satisfying to assemble because all the crucial cuts have been made for you in advance at the factory. You just add the glue and some assembly time. What's more, when someone admires the furniture that you have assembled, you can always say, "Oh that, yeah, I built that last Saturday." You never have to admit that it came from a kit. But even the best kits can be made better by ensuring that the pieces fit snuggly. This usually means touching up the components with sand papers and being careful to glue them with an ample amount of glue. If you end up with extra pieces, don't try to rationalize their presence in your package, but take the time to find out where they go. Kits are rarely sent out of the factory with extra pieces.

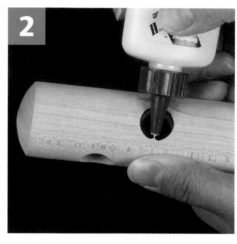

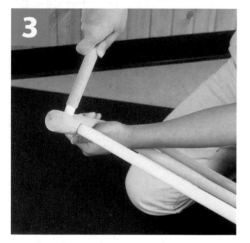

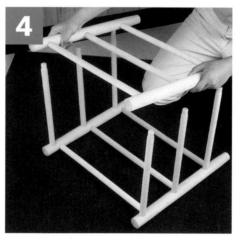

Assembling Kit Furniture

tools and materials
- Hammer ◆ Carpenter's square
- Paintbrushes or paint pads
- Rubber gloves ◆ Stain ◆ Sealer
- Furniture kit ◆ Sandpaper
- Glue and nails (if needed)

1 Start by laying out all the pieces and hardware in an exploded pattern.

2 Kits often include glue and nails. With this Shaker stool kit, rungs are glued into holes predrilled in the legs.

3 Basic kits are assembled in modular sections.

4 Square up modular sections as you assemble them, and then put the assembled sections together.

5 If the finished piece contains upholstery or some sort of fabric covering, apply stains or paint before they are installed.

6 Finish the piece after the stain or paint dries.

Assembling a Wall System

tools and materials
- Screwdriver ◆ Wall-system kit
- Hammer or rubber mallet

1 Before starting the project, read through the instructions, and make sure you have all of the components.

2 Panel sections may fit together with wooden dowel pegs. You tap them into one panel, and press them into mating panels.

3 Some panels join with threaded fasteners. The stud end mounts in one panel and fits into a predrilled hole.

4 With threaded fasteners, once the stud end is in position, you use a screwdriver to tighten the joint.

5 Assemble drawer sections with dowels and fasteners. Kits typically include full-extension drawer guides.

6 A modest-sized unit such as this can be assembled in under an hour.

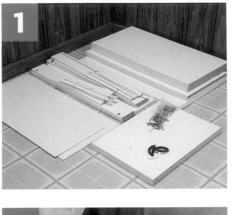

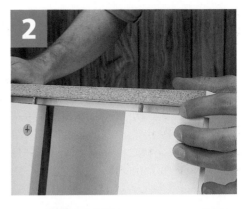

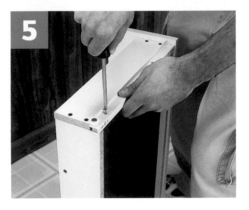

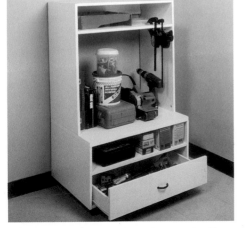

Prefab wood storage units, typically sold as knockdown kits, can be purchased with many shelf and drawer combinations.

Edge Repairs

Some knockdown kits break along the edges where panels beneath the veneer are drilled for fittings.

One solution is to make a form from wood and fill the area with epoxy. Then redrill the hole.

Refinishing Furniture

Refinishing furniture is both extremely satisfying and a great deal of work. Commit to a project only when you have enough time to finish it, and keep in mind that it's easy to underestimate how much time it will take to sand the finer details of pieces of furniture. That said, the proper tools are essential, so don't spare any expense when getting specialty, detailed sanding hand tools. Also note that older painted furniture may contain lead paint. If you sand lead paint, be sure to wear a mask and capture and dispose of the dust (don't vacuum it up, which can spread the fine lead-paint particulate). It is dangerous stuff, especially for young people with developing nervous systems. The ideal scenario is to work in a well-ventilated space away from the main living area.

Sanding

Most detail power sanders have a pointed tip to reach into tight spots. Some models are only half this size.

A belt sander is like a floor sander for furniture. The continuous belt can quickly strip and smooth a flat surface.

A random-orbit sander is ideal for finishing furniture because it can smooth opposing wood grains.

Detail Work

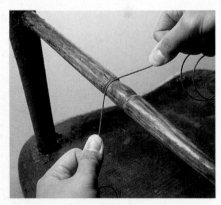

Sanding tape is like sandpaper on a string. A variety of grits are available to clean turned chair rungs and legs.

Professional refinishers may dunk an entire chair in stripper solution to remove every bit of old finish. Do-it-yourselfers have to tackle these projects one small section at a time, which can drag out a stripping project. To speed things up, use dunking where it's practical (to refurbish hardware), and use applied stripper paste, scrapers, and some specialized sanding products on the wood. A detail power sander with a pointed pad can reach into corners. Sanding tapes can handle small crevices.

Mix a solution for stripping hardware by setting up a dunking bath. Wear goggles and rubber gloves.

Heat Stripping

Use a sharp putty knife or small scraper to remove any flaking or loose finish material.

Carefully heat the surface of the finish, watching for bubbles. Keep the gun moving steadily.

As the surface layers heat up and loosen, use a scraper to work with the gun and remove the finish.

Chemical Stripping

Brush on a chemical stripper in one small area at a time. Be sure to wear gloves and safety glasses.

Spread sawdust or wood shavings over the bubbled finish to consolidate the material for removal.

Scrape off the stripper and finish. You may need small knives to clean out molding and intricate patterns.

Scraping

This long-handled draw scraper has a crooked blade. The tool is good for removing finishes on flat surfaces.

Some scrapers have several different profiles built into the blade to remove finish from flat and curved surfaces.

This triangular scraper can reach into corners, grooves, and seams. Some have interchangeable heads.

Waxing and Polishing

tools and materials

- ◆ Furniture paste wax
- ◆ Soft rag ◆ #0000 steel wool
- ◆ Electric drill with lamb's-wool pad

1 Using a #0000 steel-wool pad, apply a light, even coat of paste wax to the finish surface.

2 Rub the waxed surface down using a clean, soft rag, and buff in a circular pattern.

3 After the wax dries, use a lamb's-wool buffing attachment in an electric drill to polish the surface to a high luster.

Finishes

Before Painting

Fill all nicks, depressions, or holes with putty. Manufacturers sell color-matching putty and paint.

Before painting, take off doors, drawers, and hardware; wash everything with a mild detergent. Use a liquid deglosser on varnished cabinets to dull the shine. Scrape loose paint off painted cabinets, and sand with 180-grit sandpaper—painted hardware can be soaked in paint remover. Holes should be filled with putty and sanded flush. Prime bare wood before painting.

Painting with opaque paint? Sand filler with 220-grit sandpaper so marks won't show through.

Finishing

Sanding sealers and wood conditioners are applied to wood with large pores (such as pine) before finishing to make stains look even; sometimes sanding sealers are applied to help smooth out rough surfaces. (Sealers can prevent it from bleeding too.) Shellac and oil varnish are common sealers; there's also lacquer sanding sealer, which is used before lacquering.

Wood stains add transparent color to wood and bring out subtle grain patterns. Pigmented stains are more opaque and useful for disguising inferior stock. Aniline dyes are sometimes used to impart rich, if artificial, colors—these dyes are more translucent and generally reflect the natural color of the wood.

Gel stains, thicker and easier to use than regular wood stains, come in oil-based pigmented and water-based dye formulations. Because of their consistency, they're quite easy to handle and apply without the drips and lap marks of regular stains. The consistency makes them particularly useful if you're refinishing cabinets that are already on the wall.

Polyurethane, a synthetic varnish made from plastic resins, provides a clear, hard finish more resistant to yellowing than oil varnishes. Polyurethane dries quickly and is tough enough for floors. Both oil- and water-based varieties are fast-drying, resistant to moisture and heat, and easy to apply. They come in varying glosses, or sheens.

For better control of color absorption, especially on soft-woods, apply stain with a soft, lint-free cloth, and rub it into the wood.

Use a quality brush or a foam pad to apply stain/polyurethane combination finishes. Smooth out brush marks as you work.

If you use a natural finish like boiled linseed or tung oil, you can build up shine and keep wood clean with lemon-oil polish.

Tools

You can finish and refinish most wood surfaces with a simple hand brush, but there are some exceptions, such as a lacquer finish, that must be applied with a sprayer. Sanders have triangular heads that can dig into corners work well. One of the most important tools is a tack rag—to make sure the surface is completely clean.

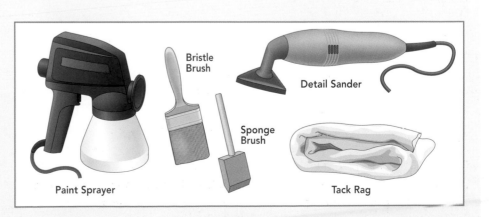

Paint Sprayer

Bristle Brush

Sponge Brush

Detail Sander

Tack Rag

8
Remodeling Primer

Remodeling Checklist

Without proper planning, remodeling can be a stressful event. Your house gets torn apart, there is dust everywhere, strangers with sharp tools show up for work either much earlier or much later than expected—and then there is the hit on your bank account. The only way to approach a major remodeling project is with a well-thoughtout plan. The goal is to do as much up-front work as possible. Establish a budget, do preliminary research on appliances and materials, and take your time in hiring the professionals. Remember: if you write the check, you are in charge, and you are the one who will live with the results.

Energy-Efficient Windows and Skylights

Cut energy costs by buying energy-efficient windows, doors, and skylights. Look for products tested by the National Fenestration Rating Council, an independent testing group. Those that meet the following requirements earn the Department of Energy's Energy Star Label.

Northern States
◆ Windows and doors must have a U-factor* of 0.35 or below.
◆ Skylights must have a U-factor* of 0.45 or below.

Middle States
◆ Windows and doors must have a U-factor* of 0.40 or below and an SHGC** rating of 0.55 or below.
◆ Skylights must have a U-factor* of 0.45 or below and an SHGC** of 0.55 or below.

Southern States
◆ Windows, doors, and skylights must have a U-factor* rating of 0.75 or below and an SHGC** of 0.40 or below.

* U-factor is a measurement of heat loss. The lower the number, the less heat lost.
** SHGC stands for Solar Heat Gain Coefficient and is a measurement of how well a product blocks heat caused by sunlight. It is a number between 0 and 1. The lower the number the more heat the product blocks.

Hiring Professionals

The quality of the contractors you choose for your remodeling project is the single greatest influence on how smoothly the process will go and how happy you will be with your finished product. It is also the area where, by far, you will be spending the most dollars. Do not be won over by a contractor who "seems nice enough." Check multiple references, interview past clients, view past work, ask at the lumberyard about his reputation, and check with the better business bureau for complaints.

Budgets

There is an adage that a remodeling budget isn't official until it is twice what you expected to spend. But getting an accurate budget is nearly impossible because you don't know what you're going to find behind the walls when you open them up, to say nothing of how costs can escalate when you finally picked out appliances and fixtures. The best approach is to make estimates and then add on a contingency figure; a 30 percent contingency is reasonable.

Contracts

Get everything in writing. That may seem obvious, but many remodelers start out with good intentions, planning to adhere to the contract, but that starts to slip as the job progresses. Before you know it, add-ons and additional labor are handled with a handshake and verbal approval. Institute a contract and work-stage-approval process (better yet, use a contractor who already has this implemented) so that all the work and expenditures are documented.

Retail Experience

The options-selection process—when you pick out your appliances, fixtures, paint colors, and floors—can be a great deal of fun. But the buying experience will be much more rewarding if you shop—at least at first—with your contractor, who will point you toward what's possible (and cost efficient) in your home.

Financing

The easiest way to finance a remodeling job is with cash or a line of credit because the funds is entirely in your control—and there is no bank inspector dropping by to approve work stages. That said, in most cases you will be borrowing money. Whatever you spend, you'll be paying back at some future time, with interest.

Appliance Ratings

Today, major appliances like freezers, refrigerators, water heaters, dishwashers, clothes washers, furnaces, and air conditioners are energy-rated for the amount of power (wattage) they use. This information appears on a large yellow "Energy Guide Label" affixed to each device. Smaller appliances may not be labeled in this manner, but their wattage rating should be listed on their packaging. The wattage rating can be used to calculate the actual operating cost of the appliance. The higher the wattage rating of the appliance, the more you will have to pay to operate it. For example, if a 4-foot long baseboard heater uses 250 watts per foot, it will require 1,000 watts to run. An 8-foot long baseboard heater will need 2,000 watts to operate. At 10¢ per kilowatt-hour (1,000 watts used by an appliance in one hour), it will cost 10¢ per hour to run the 4-foot baseboard and 20¢ per hour to operate the 8-foot baseboard. Clearly, it will cost twice as much to operate the longer unit. If the wattage of an appliance is not listed on the appliance or the packaging, then look for the voltage and current. To obtain wattage, simply multiply the two terms together: voltage times current equals power (wattage).

The energy-rating sticker on the side of this 4,500-watt water heater tells the prospective buyer approximately what he or she will be paying per year for the use of the appliance. Running a 4,500-watt water heater for one hour, at 10¢ per kilowatt-hour, would cost 4.5 x 10¢, or 45¢ per hour.

Dealing with Dust

You probably can't stop the dust generated during demolition from penetrating into other areas of your home, but you can keep the mess to a minimum. Before you begin any demolition, close off the kitchen from other rooms by hanging plastic sheeting over doorways and pass-throughs and covering heating and cooling registers. Seal the edges of the sheet with heavy duct tape. Overlap two sheets to create a flap in the door you will use to get into and out of the room. You may find it helpful to place a small fan blowing out in a kitchen window. This will help keep any dust generated from migrating to the rest of the house.

Kitchen Demolition

Even a modest kitchen remodeling can cost thousands of dollars. But you can save some money by doing the demolition work yourself. Some basic rules: shut off the water when removing plumbing fixtures; turn off the electrical power if removing light fixtures; and take note of your deconstructed room. It will provide you with an invaluable peek at how various building systems work together. This process may help you avoid future problems with your new kitchen.

Taking Apart Your Old Kitchen

tools and materials

- ◆ Screwdriver
- ◆ Basin wrench
- ◆ Putty knife
- ◆ Groove-joint pliers
- ◆ Drill with screwdriving attachment (optional)
- ◆ Reciprocating saw for tile counters
- ◆ Carpet scrap ◆ Hand truck (optional)

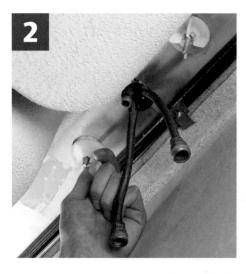

SAFETY

Dust can be more than an irritant. Asbestos, lead, and mold spores can all be contained in seemingly harmless dust. Always wear a dust mask.

1 Shut off all water lines and take the supply lines off the bottom of the faucet. Use a basin wrench to disconnect the supply line.

2 Unscrew the nuts holding the faucet assembly to the sink. Then remove the sink. Many sinks are held in place with clips. (See the Smart Tip below.)

3 To remove a dishwasher, disconnect the power and water lines to the unit. Then unscrew the screws on the underside of the countertop.

4 Slide the dishwasher out. (Protect the flooring with a carpet scrap.)

5 Countertops are held to the base cabinets with screws through cabinet corner blocks. Back out the screws, and lift up the top using a pry bar.

6 Working with a helper, lift off the countertop and remove it from the kitchen. If you don't damage it when taking it out, you can cut it to size and use it in the laundry room as a folding table or in the garage as a workbench.

7 Base cabinets are usually attached to the wall and to each other with screws, the latter driven through the cabinet stiles. Remove all of these screws, and pull out the cabinets.

Removing Stubborn Drain Fittings

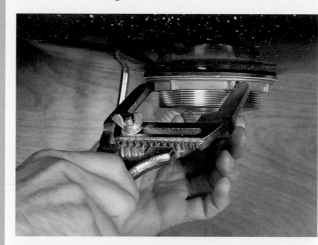

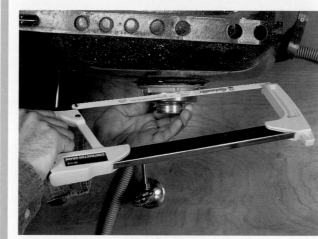

Use a spud wrench or large pliers to remove a drain's spud nut. These nuts can be sticky, so use a lubricant, or if it is safe, apply some heat with a propane torch.

If the spud nut won't budge, remove the nut by cutting it in two using a hacksaw. This chore can really skin your knuckles, so wear gloves.

SMART TIP

REMOVING RIM CLIPS
This view from underneath the sink, shows how a rim clip for a rim-style sink will look. Use a special sink-clip wrench or a nut driver with an extension to remove it.

Bathroom Demolition

Bathroom demo can get messy. The reason? Even when you shut off water lines, there is still water in traps, in toilet tanks, and in the water lines themselves. When you undo a pipe connection, some water will inevitably get on the floor, where it will mix with the dirt on the bottom of your shoes. Place old towels or scraps of carpet at the doorway for when you have to run out for tools. And have buckets and towels ready, no matter how dry your project looks initially.

Removing an Old Sink and Vanity

tools and materials

- ◆ Open-end wrench ◆ Basin wrench
- ◆ Adjustable pliers ◆ Pipe wrenches
- ◆ Pail ◆ Flashlight ◆ Wood chisel
- ◆ Putty knife or utility knife
- ◆ Power drill with screwdriver bit
- ◆ Keyhole saw or utility saw

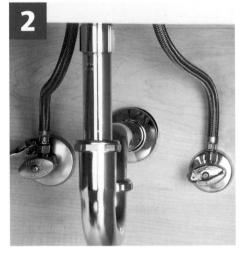

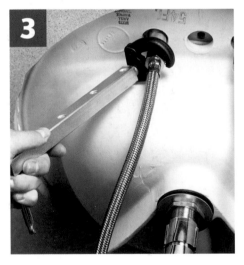

SAFETY

Use only a flashlight or a battery-powered work light to light the area below the vanity. If water drips onto a hardwired electrical light—especially a trouble light with a built-in receptacle—and causes a short, you could get hurt.

1 Turn off the water at the shutoff valves. If there are no shutoff valves, turn off the water at the main valve or water-well pressure tank.

2 Single-lever faucets come with copper tubes that extend down from the faucet valve. Remove the nuts that hold the supply risers to the wall-mounted valves.

3 On bathroom sinks with dual faucets, each faucet is connected to its shutoff valve with a separate supply riser. Remove the under-sink nuts using a basin wrench.

4 To remove the sink's waste line connection put a pail under the trap and loosen the nuts using adjustable pliers. Turn the nuts counterclockwise.

5 Remove any retaining clips or other kinds of hardware that hold the sink to the countertop. Cut the caulk seal around the sink using a sharp knife. Carefully lift it off the countertop.

6 Loosen the vanity top by removing the hold-down screws at the corners of the cabinet; then lift it off and set it aside. To quickly free the vanity cabinet, cut around the shutoff valves.

7 Remove the screws that hold the cabinet back to the wall. Then cut through any caulk or paint along the wall or floor that may hold the base in place. Pull the vanity away from the wall and discard it.

Removing a Bathtub

The easiest way to remove a tub is in one piece. Once it's free from the wall and floor, tip it on its edge, and get some help to move it. Putting an old blanket or a canvas tarp under the tub will make it easier to slide across the floor. If you have to move it down a flight of stairs, get a couple of extra people to help.

If you can't move the tub in one piece, it must be broken into smaller sections. Cast iron tubs can be broken with a mason's hammer or a sledgehammer. Steel and fiberglass tubs can be cut with a reciprocating saw. Be sure to wear eye and ear protection. Warn others in the house that you are about to engage in this demolition.

Moving Large Tubs or Showers

When you are planning the space and selecting fixtures, you should also devise a plan for removing your old tub or shower and installing the new unit. When selecting a new fixture, make sure you can carry it through the house. But if your heart is set on a unit that cannot be moved through existing hallways and doors, consider ways to move it through an outer wall. This can be as easy as removing a first-floor window or as complex as removing a section of wall on another floor.

Demolition of a Wall

It's remarkable how flimsy an interior wall can seem when you first cut into it using a reciprocating saw or poke a hole in it with a hammer, especially if it is made of drywall rather than plaster. It comes apart with remarkable ease—unless you forget to probe ahead for wires, plumbing, vents, or ducts. Tear into the wall without locating these items first, and you will have a dangerous mess on your hands. Once pipes, wires, and ducts have been located, carefully dissect the wall around them and save the slam-bam work for the sections of the wall where danger does not lurk. It's also a good idea to have a debris disposal path so that you are not dragging dusty building components across clean floors and carpets. Plastic sheets work well, but they can get slippery. Canvas cloth can be easily shaken out or washed.

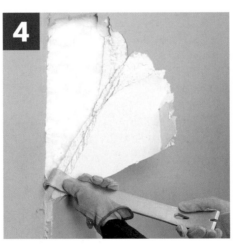

Gutting a Wall

tools and materials
- ◆ Claw hammer ◆ Shims
- ◆ Pry bar ◆ Work gloves
- ◆ Reciprocating saw
- ◆ Cold chisel (for plaster)
- ◆ Goggles & dust mask
- ◆ Power drill-driver
  (to remove drywall screws)

1 First remove the wall and ceiling trim. Once the molding is removed, pull out the nails from the backside using locking pliers.

2 Remove drywall using a hammer at first. Then switch to a wrecking bar or flat bar, and pull off the drywall. Wear a mask and safety glasses.

3 Remove drywall in large sections. During drywall demolition, a reciprocating saw with short blades works best .

4 Use a pry bar to pull the drywall sections from the wall. If you cut along the sides of the studs, it should be easy to remove large sections.

5 Once all of the drywall is off, pull out the nails along each stud using a pry bar or nail puller. Remove any screws using a drill-driver.

SAFETY

Don't cut into a wall
or ceiling without first
checking for pipes,
wiring, and ducts. Also,
cover heating registers
and exposed drains
to keep them free
of debris during
demolition.

Removing Old Vinyl Flooring

1

1 Remove baseboard and trim using a pry bar and scrap wood. Use locking pliers to pull out the nails from the back.

2

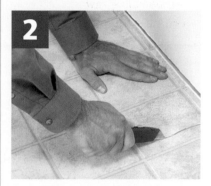

2 Cut the vinyl into strips that are 12 to 16 in. wide. Use a linoleum knife or a utility knife, and make sure to cut all the way through the flooring.

3

3 Use a flat pry bar or a wide putty knife to remove the flooring. Work one tip of the tool under a cut line and lift a corner.

Removing Ceramic Tile

Remove ceramic tile with a cold chisel, prying tiles off one by one (left). Since the drywall underneath may have to be replaced, cut away chunks with a reciprocating saw and remove the chunks whole (right). Always wear eye protection: flying pieces of tile can be dangerous.

Removing an Old Water Heater

1

1 Drain the old tank by shutting off the water supply and draining the tank with a garden hose.

2

2 Shut off the gas and undo the union fitting below the shutoff valve.

3

3 Gas heaters vent through a flue hat at the top of the heater. Remove it, and cut the water lines above the union (inset).

4

4 Pull the heater toward you and pivot it out into the room.

Resource Guide

This list of manufacturers and associations is meant to be a general guide to additional industry and product-related sources. It is not intended as a listing of products and manufacturers represented by the photographs in this book.

ELECTRICAL

EA Online

Web site: www.ea-online.com

This Web site is one of the growing number of sites that matches consumers and contractors. You can search electronically for electrical products. The location also contains numerous links to industry sites, on-line periodicals, and how-to forums.

FASTENERS & ADHESIVES

Elmer's

180 East Broad St., Columbus, OH 43215

Web site: www.elmers.com

Elmer's markets over 200 products, from school glues to home repair and woodworking products. Its range of products covers nearly every adhesive and home solution need of students, do-it-yourselfers, and even the professional contractor.

3M

3M Center, Bldg. 304-1-01,

St. Paul, MN 55144-1000

Phone: (800) 3M-HELPS / Fax: (800) 713-6329

E-mail: innovation@mmm.com

Web site: www.3M.com

3M, founded in 1902, started as a mining and abrasives company, but it now makes thousands of products in manufacturing facilities located in more than 60 countries. Among 3M's developments are masking tape, cellophane tape, waterproof sandpaper, and magnetic sound recording and videotape.

HEATING AND COOLING

AHAM

1111 19th Street, NW, Suite 402,

Washington, DC 20036

Phone: (202) 872-5955 / Fax: (202) 872-9354

Web site: www.aham.org

AHAM—the Association of Home Appliance Manufacturers—provides programs and services regarding home appliances, including data compilation, technical standards development, and public information. Its Web site contains information on room air conditioners and dehumidifiers, as well as most other major appliances.

Lennox Industries

2100 Lake Park Blvd., Richardson TX 75080

Phone: (800) 9-LENNOX

Web site: www.lennox.com

Lennox, founded in 1985, is a premium manufacturer of residential and commercial heating and air-conditioning equipment and related products. It is recognized as the leader in high-efficiency comfort conditioning. Lennox markets its products via one-step distribution, directly to its network of 6,000 independent dealers.

INSULATION

North American Insulation Manufacturers Association (NAIMA)

44 Canal Center Plaza, Suite 310

Alexandria, VA 22314

Phone: (703) 684-0084 / Fax: (703) 684-0427

E-mail: insulation@naima.org

Web site: www.naima.org

NAIMA is a trade association of North American manufacturers of fiberglass, rock wool, and slag wool insulation products. NAIMA's role is to promote energy efficiency and environmental preservation through the use of these products, and to encourage their safe production and use. Visit the Web site for publications on application and benefits of these products.

Owens Corning

1 Owens Corning Parkway, Toledo, OH 43659

Phone: (800) Get-Pink

E-mail: answers@owenscorning.com

Web site: www.owenscorning.com

Owens Corning offers a full array of products and systems for the home, including roofing, exterior, insulating, and acoustical. Call the toll-free number for free information.

MASONRY

Brick Industry Association

11490 Commerce Park Dr.,

Reston, VA 20191-1525

Phone: (703) 620-0010 / Fax: (703) 620-3928

E-mail: brickinfo@big.org

Web site: www.brickinfo.org

The Brick Industry Association is a national trade association representing brick manufacturers and distributors in the U.S. Write or call for a free catalog listing various do-it-yourself brochures and videos on brick.

Prosoco

3741 Greenway Circle, Lawrence, KS 66046

Phone: (800) 255-4255 / Fax: (785) 830-9797

Web site: www.prosoco.com

Prosoco is a custom formulator of specialty cleaners and protective treatments for masonry and concrete, designed to improve their appearance and performance. Products and services developed by Prosoco have been used on the U.S. Capitol, the World Trade Plaza, and the Smithsonian, among many others.

REMODELING GUIDE

American Arbitration Association

335 Madison Ave., 10th Fl.,
New York, NY 10017-4605
Phone: (800) 778-7879 / Fax: (212) 716-5905
Web site: www.adr.org
This organization is available to resolve a wide range of disputes through mediation, arbitration, elections, and other out-of-court settlement procedures. It provides a forum for the hearing of disputes in 37 offices nationwide, using a roster of 17,000 impartial experts.

Council of Better Business Bureaus

4200 Wilson Blvd., Suite 800,
Arlington, VA 22203-1838
Phone: (703) 276-0100 / Fax: (703) 525-8277
Web site: www.bbb.org
The mission of all local Better Business Bureaus is to promote and foster the highest ethical relationship between businesses and the public through voluntary self-regulation, consumer and business education, and service excellence. The CBBB is the umbrella organization for the 132 local bureaus, supported by more than 250,000 local business members nationwide.

International Code Council (ICC)

5203 Leesburg Pike, Suite 600,
Falls Church, VA 22041
Phone: (888) ICC-SAFE (422-7233)
Web site: www.iccsafe.org
The ICC is a nonprofit organization that provides a comprehensive set of national model construction codes. The founders of the ICC are Building Officials and Code Administrators International, Inc. (BOCA), International Conference of Building Officials (ICBO), and Southern Building Code Congress International, Inc. (SBCCI). Now you can direct all of your questions and concerns about building regulations to one forum, the ICC, for consideration.

National Association of the Remodeling Industry (NARI)

780 Lee Street, Suite 200
Des Plaines, IL 60016
Phone: (800) 611-6274
Web site: www.remodeltoday.com

Members of NARI are full-service contractors, design-build firms, manufacturers, suppliers, distributors, subcontractors, lenders, and other related professionals in the remodeling field. NARI certification provides the industry with a formalized standard of expertise. Its Web site allows you to search for pros in your area.

Carpet and Rug Institute

P.O. Box 2048, 310 Holiday Ave.,
Dalton, GA 30720-2048
Phone: (800) 882-8846 / Fax: (706) 278-8835
Web site: www.carpet-rug.com
CRI provides material—some items free of charge and some at a small charge—for consumers, including guidelines for carpet/rug selection, installation, daily maintenance and long-term care, and information on carpet's role in indoor air quality and the environment.

Crain Cutter Company

1155 Wrigley Way,
Milpitas, CA 95035-5426
Phone: (408) 946-6100 / Fax: (408) 946-4268
Web site: www.craintools.com
Crain Cutter produces tools for the floorcovering trade, such as stretchers and kickers used to install carpeting. Product catalogs are available.

National Oak Flooring Manufacturers Assoc.

P.O. Box 3009,
Memphis, TN 38173-0009
Phone: (901) 526-5016 / Fax: (901) 526-7022
Web site: www.nofma.org
NOFMA is the main trade association for hardwood flooring manufacturing and grading. Its Web site includes information on estimating, installing, refinishing, and repairing hardwood floors. You can order how-to flooring pamphlets.

Pittsburgh Corning Corporation

800 Presque Isle Dr., Pittsburgh, PA 15239
Phone: (724) 327-6100 / Fax: (724) 325-9704
Web site: www.pittsburghcorning.com
Pittsburgh Corning provides a full line of glass-block products and accessories, including fully-assembled LightWise windows and Pittsburgh Corning glass-block shower systems. Call the toll-free number to reach the Glass Block Resource Center with distributor locator, product information, and answers to frequently asked questions regarding products and installation.

Resource Guide

SAFETY & SECURITY

AD • AS

2728 S. Cole Rd., Boise, ID 83709

Phone: (800) 208-2020

Web site: www.ad-as.com

AD • AS (Accessible Design–Adjustable Systems Inc.) makes height-adjustable sink systems, height-adjustable cooktop systems, height-adjustable wall cabinets, ergonomic office furniture, accessible computer furniture, library furniture, and rehab furniture. Call for a free catalog.

American Red Cross

Public Inquiry Office, 11th Floor,

1621 N. Kent St., Arlington, VA 22209

Phone: (703) 248-4222

E-mail: info@usa.redcross.org

Web site: www.redcross.org

The American Red Cross provides support for people involved in natural disasters and wars worldwide. Its Web site provides information on subjects such as repairing a flooded home, the risks of mudslides, how to prepare for a hurricane, as well as up-to-date information on Red Cross activities throughout the world.

ASTM

100 Barr Harbor Dr.,

West Conshohocken, PA 19428-2959

Phone: (610) 832-9585 / Fax: (610) 832-9555

Web site: www.astm.org

ASTM (the American Society for Testing and Materials) develops standards for a wide variety of materials–for example, so that light bulbs from different manufacturers all fit in one kind of socket. The Web site contains safety standards.

Federal Emergency Management Agency (FEMA)

500 C Street, SW, Washington, DC 20472

Web site: www.fema.gov

FEMA is the federal agency that helps people before, during, and after natural disasters. FEMA runs several consumer education campaigns focusing on safety planning, makes financial assistance available to states, administers both national flood and crime insurance programs, and provides advice on building codes and safe building sites.

Honeywell

101 Columbia Rd., Morristown, NJ 07962

Phone: (800) 421-2133 or (973) 455-2000

Fax: (973) 455-4807

Web site: www.honeywell.com

Honeywell produces a wide range of residential and commercial heating and cooling controls and security systems. Honeywell's diversified subsidiaries also produce a variety of other products for your home, office, and automobile.

TILE

The Tile Council of America

100 Clemson Research Blvd.,

Anderson, SC 29625

Phone: (864) 646-8453 / Fax: (864) 646-2821

Web site: www.tileusa.com

The Tile Council of America provides technical assistance and literature to the tile industry. To receive technical assistance in reference to tile installation and maintenance, visit its Web site.

TOOLS

Craftsman Tools (Sears, Roebuck & Co.)

3333 Beverly Rd., Hoffman Estates, IL 60179

Phone: (800) 349-4358

Web site: www.craftsman.com

Craftsman has been manufacturing hand and power tools for the professional carpenter, mechanic, and do-it-yourselfers for over 100 years. The company also makes an extensive line of tool storage boxes from work-site portables to large roll-away drawer sets. All of its extensive line of mechanic's hand tools come with a lifetime guarantee, and all can be purchased at Sears stores nationwide and at the Craftsman Web site.

Hitachi Power Tools

3950 Steve Reynolds Blvd., Norcross, GA 30093

Phone: (800) 829-4752 / Fax: (770) 279-4293

Web site: www.hitachi.com

Hitachi makes a wide range of hand-held power tools and bench tools such as table saws for working with wood, metal, and concrete. It also manufactures a line of pneumatic tools, such as nailers and staplers, and the air compressors to power them. Call for more information or to locate a dealer or service center near you.

Makita USA

4930 Northam St., La Mirada, CA 90638

Phone: (714) 522-8088

Web site: www.makitausa.com

Makita manufacturers portable power tools, including saws, planers, drills, hammers, grinders, sanders, as well as pneumatic tools and outdoor power equipment. The U.S. operation includes over 1000 authorized service centers and a dealer network handling Makita's 65 tool models, which are manufactured in Buford, Georgia.

Porter-Cable Corporation

4825 Hwy. 45 North, P.O. Box 2468

Jackson, TN 38302-2468

Phone: (800) 4US-TOOL / Fax: (713) 660-9525

Web site: www.porter-cable.com

Porter-Cable, a subsidiary of Pentair, Inc., is a leading manufacturer of portable electric and cordless power tools, nailers, staplers, compressors, and related accessories for the professional woodworking, commercial and residential construction, plumbing, and electrical markets.

Ryobi North America

1424 Pearman Dairy Rd., Anderson, SC 29625

Phone: (800) 525-2579

Web site: www.ryobi.com

Ryobi produces portable and benchtop power tools for contractors and do-it-yourselfers. It also manufactures a line of lawn and garden tools. Call its toll-free customer service line for free literature, or go on-line for customer service, a power tool forum, warranty registration, and sales of selected products and accessories.

The Stanley Works

1000 Stanley Drive, New Britain, CT 06053

Phone: (800) STANLEY

Web site: www.stanleyworks.com

The Stanley Works, founded in 1843, provides a line of hand and power tools for contractors and homeowners. Its specialty products include a series of ergonomically designed products and a line of extra-durable contractor tools for the job site. For information, call its toll-free information line or visit the Web site.

TRIMWORK

Cumberland Woodcraft Company

P.O. Drawer 609, Carlisle, PA 17013-0609

Phone: (800) 367-1884

Web site: www.cumberlandwoodcraft.com

This firm is one of the nation's largest and oldest manufacturers of period architectural millwork in the form of wall niches, moldings, ornaments, and wallcoverings. Their line of over 350 products include mantlepieces, bars, sculptural figures, and complete gazebos. All products are made from premium grades of solid, kiln-dried woods for minimum shrinkage, mainly poplar and oak, that are sealed and finished on-site.

White River Hardwoods—Woodworks Inc.

1197 Happy Hollow Rd.,

Fayetteville, AR 72701

Phone: (800) 558-0119 / Fax: (501) 444-0406

Web site: www.mouldings.com

White River has manufactured architectural molding since 1981. It specializes in decorative hardwood moldings and authentic hand-carved wood carvings: over 450 profiles with five different price ranges. Available nationwide through lumberyards and fine millwork houses. Contact the company for samples, design assistance, free brochures, and various catalogs.

WALLS & CEILINGS

Brewster Wallcovering Company

67 Pacella Park Dr., Randolph, MA 02368

Phone: (800) 366-1701 / Fax: (781) 963-8805

Web site: www.ewallpaper.com

Brewster manufactures wallpaper, borders, fabrics, and accessories including valances, shower curtains, and chair pads. Free consumer brochures, how-to-decorate videos, and referral to local retail stores is available by phone or by visiting its Web site.

BPB America, Inc.

5301 West Cypress St., Suite 300

Tampa, FL 33607-1766

Web site: www.bpb-na.com

BPB Celotex produces consistently high-quality gypsum board, as well as tile backer board, interior ceiling board, and related gypsum products for use in residential and commercial construction, plus specially formulated products for fire-resistance-rated designs.

Chicago Metallic

4849 S. Austin Ave., Chicago, IL 60638

Phone: (800) 323-7164 / Fax: (800) 222-3744

Web site: www.chicago-metallic.com

Chicago Metallic produces suspended ceiling grids and panels in several materials, including fiberglass, vinyl-covered gypsum, and stamped metal. Its roofing products include Shingle Shield roof and deck cleaner and Shingle Shield zinc strips. Call the samples and literature hotline listed above to request brochures.

Glossary

Actual dimensions The exact measurements of a piece of lumber, pipe, or masonry. See "Nominal dimensions."

Aerator The unit screwed onto the end of a faucet to control splashing.

Ampere (amp) A unit of measurement describing the rate of electrical flow.

Anchor bolt A bolt set in concrete that is used to fasten lumber, brackets, or hangers to concrete or masonry walls.

Apron Architectural trim beneath a window stool; also, the wider end of a drive that abuts the street.

Baluster One of the vertical supports for a handrail.

Battens Narrow wood strips that typically cover vertical joints between siding boards.

Bay window A window that projects from a wall, creating a niche in the interior.

Beam A steel or wood framing member installed horizontally to support part of a structure's load.

Bearing wall A wall that provides support to the framing above.

Bevel An angled surface not at 90 degrees, typically cut into the edge of a piece of lumber.

Blocking Lumber added between studs, joists, rafters, or other framing members to provide a nailing surface, additional strength, or as a fire stop to keep fire from spreading.

Board foot A measurement of wood by volume, equivalent to 1 foot square and 1 inch thick.

Bottom plate The horizontal framing member at the base of a wall.

Bridging Lumber or metal installed in an X-shape between floor joists to stabilize and position the joists.

Btu British thermal unit; the standard measurement of heat energy.

Cable Two or more insulated wires inside a sheathing of plastic or metal.

Carcass The basic case of a cabinet.

Casing The exposed trim around windows and doors.

Check valve A valve that allows water to flow in only one direction.

Circuit breaker A protective device that opens a circuit automatically when a current overload occurs. It can be reset manually.

Cleanout A removable plug in a trap or drainpipe, which allows easier access for removing blockages.

Cleat A block used to support wood braces or other members.

Code The rules set down by local or county governments that specify minimum building practices.

Column A vertical support in a building frame, made of wood, metal, or concrete.

Conduit Metal or plastic tubing designed to enclose electrical wires.

Control joints Joints tooled into the surface that make concrete crack in planned locations.

Cornice Ornamental trim at the meeting of roof and wall (exterior) or at the top of a wall (interior).

Coped joint A curved cut on a piece of trim that makes the reverse image of the piece it must butt against; made with a coping saw.

CPVC Chlorinated polyvinyl chloride; a plastic used to make hot-water pipe.

Curing Providing proper moisture to a concrete slab to reduce cracking and shrinkage and develop strength.

Deflection The bending of wood due to live and dead loads.

Dormer A shed- or doghouse-like structure that projects from a roof, built to add space to an attic.

Drywall Gypsum sandwiched between treated paper, used as an interior wall covering. Also called gypsum board or wallboard.

D-W-V Drain-waste-vent; the system of pipes and fittings used to carry away wastewater.

Easement The legal right for one person to cross or use another person's land.

Eaves The lower part of a roof that projects beyond the supporting walls to create an overhang.

Escutcheon A metal plate that covers the hole in the wall around a pipe or faucet.

Façade The exterior face of a building.

Face brick A type of brick used when a consistent appearance is needed.

Face-nailing Nailing perpendicularly through the surface of lumber.

Fascia One-by or two-by trim piece nailed onto the end grain or tail end of a rafter to form part of a cornice or soffit.

Finial The decorative element on top of a post.

Fish tape Flexible metal strip used to draw wires and cables through walls and conduits.

Furring Narrow one-by or two-by wood strips used to create space—for example, between ceilings and joists or between insulated walls and masonry.

Fuse A safety device designed to protect circuits; it shuts off the current in case of overload or short circuit.

Gasket Resilient material that seals joints against leaks, such as between door and jamb or pipe and fitting.

Gable end The triangular wall section under each end of a gable roof.

Girder A horizontal wood or steel member used to support some aspect of a framed structure. Also called a beam.

Ground The connection between electrical circuits or equipment and the earth.

Ground-fault circuit interrupter (GFCI) A device that detects a ground fault or electrical line leakage and immediately shuts down power to that circuit.

Grout A binder and filler applied to the joints between ceramic tile.

Gypsum board See "Drywall."

Hardwood Wood that comes from deciduous trees, such as oak and maple.

Header The thick horizontal member that runs above rough openings, like doors and windows, in a building's frame.

HVAC Heating, ventilating, and air-conditioning.

Jack stud A stud that runs from the bottom plate to the underside of a header. Also called a trimmer.

Jamb The upright surface forming the side in an opening, as for a door, window, or fireplace.

Joist Horizontal framing lumber placed on edge to support subfloors or hold up ceilings.

Joist hanger Bracket used to strengthen the connection between a joist and a piece of lumber into which it butts.

Junction box Metal or plastic box inside which all standard wire splices and wiring connections must be made.

Knockdown Having precut and prefit construction components; usually refers to unassembled furniture.

Lath Wood strips or metal mesh used as a foundation for plaster or stucco.

Lattice Thin strips of wood crossed to make a pattern for a trellis or arbor.

Leader The downspout in a gutter system; also, the duct that sends hot air to an outlet.

Ledger A horizontal board attached to a beam or other member and used as a shelf-like support for lumber that butts against the beam.

Mastic A thick, pasty adhesive.

Miter A joint in which two boards are joined at angles (usually 45 degrees) to form a corner.

Miter box An open-ended box with precut guides for angled or square saw cuts.

Mortar A mixture used to bind masonry or as a bedding for tile.

Mortise-and-tenon Wood joint where a protrusion (tenon) fits into a recess (mortise), usually at a right angle.

Nominal dimensions In lumber, the premilling measurement for which a piece of lumber is named (i.e., 2x4); in masonry, the measured dimensions of a masonry unit plus one mortar joint.

Oriented-strand board (OSB) Panel material made of wood strands purposely aligned for strength and bonded by phenolic resin.

Particleboard Panel material made from wood flakes held together by resin.

Partition wall A non-load-bearing wall built to divide up interior space.

Penny (Abbreviation: d.) Unit of measurement for nail length, such as a 10d nail, which is 3 inches long.

Pigtail A short piece of wire used to complete a circuit inside a box.

Pitch Loosely, the slope or angle of a roof; technically, the rise of a roof over its span.

Plumb Vertically straight. A line 90 degrees to a level line.

Prehung door A door that's already set in a jamb, with hinges (and sometimes a lockset) preinstalled, ready to be installed in a rough opening.

Pressure treated Wood that has preservatives forced into it under pressure.

PVC Polyvinyl chloride; a plastic used to make drain and vent pipe.

R-value "R" is the measure of a substance's resistance to heat flow. An R-value is a number assigned to insulation. The higher the number, the better the insulation.

Raceway Surface wiring system that allows the addition of outlets, switches, and fixtures on top of a finished wall rather than inside.

Rebar Short for "reinforcement bar." Metal bars laid in a grid used to reinforce concrete.

Relief valve A safety device that automatically releases water due to excessive pressure or temperature.

Ridge The horizontal crest of a roof.

Rip To cut wood in the same direction as the grain.

Riser In plumbing, a water-supply pipe that carries water vertically; in carpentry, the vertical part of a stair installed on edge, across the front of the step.

Scarf joint Joint formed when the ends of two pieces of lumber meet in the same plane at a 45-degree angle.

Screeding Using a straight 2x4 to strike off excess concrete poured into a form.

Seat cut (rafter) The horizontal cut in a bird's mouth that fits on a top panel or horizontal framing member.

Setback A local building code that requires structures to be built a certain distance from the street, sidewalk, or property line.

Sheathing Panel material, typically plywood, applied to the outside of a structure. Siding is installed over it.

Shim A thin wedge of plastic or wood used as blocking to level or plumb doors, windows, and framing lumber.

Sill The horizontal two-by lumber attached directly to the masonry foundation. It supports the building's walls. Also, the piece of wood at the bottom of a window frame, typically angled to shed water.

Slope The rise of a roof over its run, expressed as the number of inches of rise per unit of run (usually 12 inches). For example: 6-in-12 means a roof rises 6 inches for every 12 inches of run.

Stringer On stairs, the diagonal boards that support the treads and risers.

Stud Vertical two-by lumber that extends from the bottom plate to the top plate of a wall.

Subfloor The flooring underneath a finished floor, usually plywood or OSB decking installed on floor joists or sleepers.

Toenailing Driving a nail at an angle into the face of a board so that it penetrates another board beneath or above it.

Top plate The horizontal two-by board nailed to the top of wall studs.

Transformer A device designed to convert the voltage in a circuit to a different level.

Trap The water-filled curved pipe that prevents sewer gas from entering the house through the drainage network.

Trim One-by lumber used as siding corner boards or as finish materials around windows and doors, under eaves, or other architectural elements.

Valve seat The part of the valve into which a washer or other piece fits, stopping the flow of water.

Veneer A thin piece or section of wood or masonry.

Volt The unit of measure of electrical force.

Water hammer A knocking in water pipes caused by a sudden change in pressure after a faucet or water valve shuts off.

Watt Unit of measurement of electrical power required or consumed by a fixture or appliance.

Index

Index

Photo Credits

All interior photography by John Parsekian/CH or Brian C. Nieves/CH, unless otherwise noted.

page 2 davidduncanlivingston.com Brian Vanden Brink **page 11** Merle Henkenius **page 13** *both* Merle Henkenius **page 17** *top* Merle Henkenius **page 22** courtesy of Paslode **page 28** Bob Greenspan, stylist: Susan Andrews **page 29** Freeze Frame Studio/CH **page 31** *top and middle rows* Don Wong/CH **page 32** Jessie Walker **page 33** *bottom left and right* Merle Henkenius **page 34** *bottom left and right* Freeze Frame Studio/CH **page 36** Freeze Frame Studio/CH **page 39** *top* carolynbates.com, designer: Milford Cushman, The Cushman Design Group, Inc. **page 41** *all* Freeze Frame Studio/CH **page 42** Mark Samu **page 47** Jesse Walker **page 48** *all* Merle Henkenius **page 49** *all left* Merle Henkenius *all right* courtesy of Honeywell **page 50** *all* Merle Henkenius **page 51** courtesy of Carrier Corp **page 52** *all* Merle Henkenius **page 53** *top left* courtesy of Custom Building Products *top right* Freeze Frame Studio/CH **page 54** *all* Merle Henkenius **page 64** courtesy of Merillat **page 65** Merle Henkenius **pages 66-68** *all* Merle Henkenius **page 69** *top right* Freeze Frame Studio/CH *all others* Merle Henkenius **page 70** *all* Merle Henkenius **page 71** *top* Freeze Frame Studio/CH *bottom* Merle Henkenius **page 72** *all* Merle Henkenius **page 73** Freeze Frame Studio/CH **pages 74-86** *all* Merle Henkenius **page 87** *bottom left and right* Merle Henkenius **pages 88-89** *all* Merle Henkenius **page 91** *all* Merle Henkenius **page 92** Jessie Walker **page 105** *all* courtesy of Malibu Lighting/Intermatic Inc. **pages 106-107** *all* Merle Henkenius **page 120** Todd Caverly **pages 122-123** *bottom row* courtesy of Interactive Technologies, Inc. **page 129** *left column* Stephen Munz **page 135** *top and bottom left* courtesy of Closet Maid **page 138** *all* Neal Barrett/CH **page 139** *all top* Neal Barrett/CH *bottom left* Neal Barrett/CH *bottom right* Gary David Gold/CH **pages 140-141** *all* Neal Barrett/CH **page 145** *bottom left* Neal Barrett/CH **pages 146-149** *all* Freeze Frame Studio/CH **page 154** *bottom left and right* Jim Roberson **page 156** Mark Samu **page 157** Freeze Frame Studio/CH **page 159** *bottom* Freeze Frame Studio/CH **page 160** *all* Freeze Frame Studio/CH **page 161** *all* Merle Henkenius **pages 162-164** *all* Freeze Frame Studio/CH **page 165** *left column and top row* Freeze Frame Studio/CH *middle and bottom rows* Merle Henkenius

Contributing Illustrators: Frank Rorbach, Clarke Barre, Robert Strauch, Charles Von Vooren, Ian Warpole, Tony Davis, Rob Hildebrand, Greg Maxson, Thomas Moore, and Robert LaPointe.

METRIC EQUIVALENTS

Length

1 inch	25.4mm
1 foot	0.3048m
1 yard	0.9144m
1 mile	1.61km

Area

1 square inch	645mm²
1 square foot	0.0929m²
1 square yard	0.8361m²
1 acre	4046.86m²
1 square mile	2.59km²

Volume

1 cubic inch	16.3870cm³
1 cubic foot	0.03m³
1 cubic yard	0.77m³

Common Lumber Equivalents

Sizes: Metric cross sections are so close to their U.S. sizes, as noted below, that for most purposes they may be considered equivalents.

Dimensional lumber	1 x 2	19 x 38mm
	1 x 4	19 x 89mm
	2 x 2	38 x 38mm
	2 x 4	38 x 89mm
	2 x 6	38 x 140mm
	2 x 8	38 x 184mm
	2 x 10	38 x 235mm
	2 x 12	38 x 286mm
Sheet sizes	4 x 8 ft.	1200 x 2400mm
	4 x 10 ft.	1200 x 3000mm
Sheet thicknesses	¼ in.	6mm
	⅜ in.	9mm
	½ in.	12mm
	¾ in.	19 mm
Stud/joist spacing	16 in. o.c.	400mm o.c.
	24 in. o.c.	600mm o.c.

Capacity

1 fluid ounce	29.57mL
1 pint	473.18mL
1 quart	0.95L
1 gallon	3.79L

Weight

1 ounce	28.35g
1 pound	0.45kg

Temperature

Fahrenheit = Celsius x 1.8 + 32
Celsius = Fahrenheit - 32 x 5⁄9

Nail Size & Length

Penny Size	Nail Length
2d	1"
3d	1¼"
4d	1½"
5d	1¾"
6d	2"
7d	2¼"
8d	2½"
9d	2¾"
10d	3"
12d	3¼"
16d	3½"

Have a home gardening, decorating, or improvement project? Look for these and other fine Creative Homeowner books wherever books are sold.

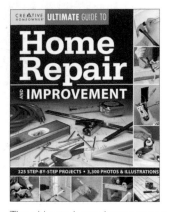

The ultimate home-improvement reference manual. Over 300 step-by-step projects. 608 pp; 9"×10⁷/₈"
BOOK#: 267870

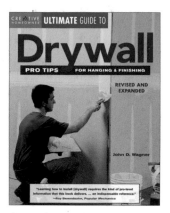

A complete guide covering all aspects of drywall. Over 325 color illustrations.160 pp.; 8¹/₂"×10⁷/₈"
BOOK #: 278320

Guide to designing and building decks. Over 650 color photos. 288 pp.; 8¹/₂"×10⁷/₈"
BOOK #: 277168

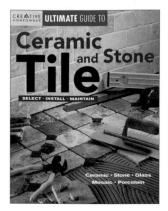

Everything you need to know about setting ceramic tile. Over 450 photos. 224 pp.; 8¹/₂"×10⁷/₈"
BOOK#: 277532

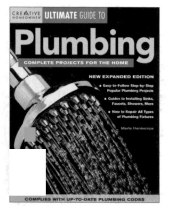

The complete manual for plumbing projects. Over 800 color photos and illustrations. 288 pp.; 8¹/₂"×10⁷/₈"
BOOK#: 278200

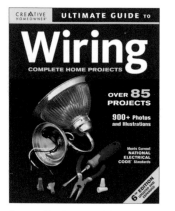

Best-selling house-wiring manual. Over 840 color photos and illustrations. 320 pp.; 8¹/₂"×10⁷/₈"
BOOK#: 278242

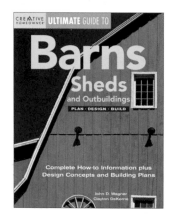

Plan, construct, and finish out-buildings. 850+ color photos and illustrations. 240 pp.; 8¹/₂"×10⁷/₈"
BOOK#: 277812

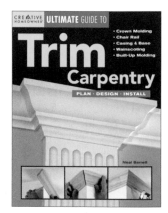

Step-by-step photos show the correct way to install trimwork. Over 500 color photos and illustrations. 208 pp., 8¹/₂"×10⁷/₈"
BOOK#: 277516

How to create kitchen style like a pro. Over 500 photos and illos. 224 pp.; 8¹/₂"×10⁷/₈"
BOOK #: 279415

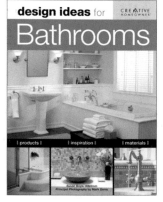

All you need to know about designing a bath. Over 475 color photos. 224 pp., 8¹/₂"×10⁷/₈"
BOOK #: 279268

An impressive guide to landscape design and plant selection. More than 950 color photos. 384 pp.; 9"×10"
BOOK #: 274610

Lavishly illustrated with portraits of over 100 flowering plants; more than 500 photos. 208 pp.; 9"×10"
BOOK #: 274032